Beyond the Rhetoric

Essays in Africa's
Developmental Challenges

Published by
Adonis & Abbey Publishers Ltd
P.O. Box 43418
London
SE11 4XZ
http://www.adonis-abbey.com

First Edition, February 2006

Copyright © Chinua Akukwe

British Library Cataloguing-in-Publication Data

A catalogue record for this book is available from the British Library
ISBN 1-905068-23-9

The moral right of the author has been asserted

Cover Design Mega Graphix

Printed and bound in Great Britain

Beyond the Rhetoric

Essays in Africa's Developmental Challenges

By

Chinua Akukwe

Adonis & Abbey
Publishers Ltd

ACKOWLEDGEMENT

I thank Jideofor Adibe and his editors at the Adonis & Abbey Publishers, London, United Kingdom for their wonderful editorial reviews and logistics for the publication of this book. Jideofor Adibe provided expert guidance on choice of materials for this book and flawlessly coordinated the logistics from editorial reviews to the publication of the book.

I am very grateful to George Nubo, the editor in chief of the THE PERSPECTIVE Magazine, based in Atlanta, United States for his long-term support of my writings on development issues in Africa. I thank Chuck Odili, the publisher of NIGERIAWORLD.COM for his early and continuous of my writings on African issues. I thank Shane Tasker the web-editor of the WORLDPRESSS.ORG for his continued attention to development issues in Africa. I also thank Terri Schure, the editor-in-chief/founder of WORLDPRESS.ORG for her continued support and encouragement. I also extend my gratitude to Chuks Iloegbunam, one of Nigeria's most celebrated journalists and a columnist for the Vanguard Newspapers in Nigeria for his support, encouragement and expert advice on development issues in Nigeria and other parts of Africa.

I thank the editors of all journals, newspapers, web portals, radio and television programs in the United States, Africa and other parts of the world who had printed my articles on development issues in Africa. Their role is critical to international development remedial efforts in Africa. Their organizations are also powerful bulwarks against repeating mistake made during more than forty years of development assistance in Africa.

I thank Melvin Foote, the President and Chief Executive Officer of the Constituency for Africa for his long term service as an advocate for African issues in the United States. Dr. Mohammad Akhter, the president and chief executive officer of the Interaction, Washington, DC is a pioneer of how medical doctors can use their training in social medicine to become recognized leaders in international development. Dr. Akhter as the former executive director of the American Public Health Association and as a senior associate dean for international public health at Howard University is well known for his firm conviction on the link between effective healthcare and sustainable development. I also thank Dr. Sidi Jammeh, the former Chairman of the Africa Society of the World Bank and International Monetary Fund for his distinguished service as a strong promoter of African representation in top leadership positions in multilateral institutions and his work in rural development in various countries in Africa. I also extend my gratitude to Honorable George Haley, the former US Ambassador to the Gambia and the younger bother of the celebrated journalist/novelist, Alex Haley. George Haley after more than 30 years of direct experience on Africa issues believes that the best years are still ahead.

As a firm believer in Africa's capacity to provide leadership on its identified development issues, I acknowledge the work ongoing in various African-based institutions, professional organizations and government agencies to make the continent a better place.

Dedication

This book is dedicated to individuals and organizations in Africa, the West and other parts of the world working round the clock to solve development challenges in Africa.

TABLE OF CONTENTS

PART I
AFRICA AND THE WEST: BEYOND THE RHETORIC OF DEVELOPMENT

PART II
AFRICA'S HOME GROWN DEVELOPMENT INITIATIVES

PART III
LEADERSHIP ISSUES IN AFRICA

FOREWORD

I am pleased that Dr. Chinua Akukwe has written this book, *Beyond the Rhetoric: Essays on Africa's Development Challenges.* This book is timely as the international community comes to grip with the monumental development challenges in Africa. According to the United Nations, Africa is on course to miss most of the 2015 Millennium Development Goals. These development challenges are not insurmountable as noted by Dr. Akukwe in many essays in the book. However, to overcome these challenges, Dr Akukwe notes the need for effective leadership, priority setting, and, mobilization of talent abundant in Africa.

In my current role as the president and chief executive officer of the American Council for Voluntary International Action (InterAction), Washington, DC, the membership entity for US-based non-governmental organizations that provide assistance in developing regions, including Africa, I know first hand the critical importance of genuine partnership between donor and recipient organizations. Without genuine partnership, a clear understanding of the goals and objectives, and, a clear articulation of projected outcomes, it is difficult to achieve sustainable development.

I am pleased that a major theme of this book is the need for genuine partnership between Africa and its development partners. In my nearly 40 years of health and development practice, moving from working in an urban slum health clinic in Pakistan to deanship of a community-based public health school in a rural area to leadership of health departments in urban centers in America, I know first hand that the key to meeting development challenges is to nurture and sustain genuine partnerships with target communities. As a former executive director of the American Public Health Association and a senior associate dean for international public health at the Howard University, Washington, DC, I know that sustainable international development assistance requires the recipient nation or community to articulate its development priorities and convince external partners to meet identified need. Thus, I welcome Dr. Akukwe's close attention to the issue of strong technical leadership from Africa on development assistance in this book.

Dr. Chinua Akukwe has a distinguished career that is still unfolding. His professional experiences qualify him as a credible observer of development assistance in Africa. Dr. Akukwe grew up in Nigeria and completed his medical training in Nigeria. Our paths crossed when as the Commissioner of Health, Washington, DC, I hired him to serve as the scientific coordinator of the US Congress mandated Initiative to Reduce Infant Mortality in Minority Populations of the United States, starting from Washington, DC. Some of the major causes of disparate infant mortality rates between whites and blacks in Washington, DC resided outside the medical arena. These issues revolve around poverty, lack of employment opportunities, low levels of education among women, and chronic health conditions due to stressful experiences in life before onset of pregnancy. Without addressing these social issues, the rate of infant deaths will not come down. These social issues are also prevalent in developing countries.

Dr. Akukwe has gone on to become the Vice Chairman of the Executive Committee and Governing Board of the National Council for International Health (NCIH) now known as the Global Health Council, Washington, DC. In this position, he initiated the successful transformation of NCIH to the now widely acclaimed Global Health Council. He is a member of the Board of Directors of the Constituency for Africa, one of the most widely respected advocacy organizations in United States. He has served as a member of the International Human Rights Committee of the American Public Health Association. He is the Chairman of the Technical Advisory Board of the George Washington University Africa Center for Health and Security, Washington, DC. This Center is focusing on developing genuine partnership between African institutions, governments and civil society. Today, Dr. Chinua Akukwe is well known for his work on health and development issues in Africa. This is in addition to his stature as a global health expert.

I recommend this book to students and scholars of development in Africa. I also recommend the book to policy makers in Africa, the West and other parts of the World who deal with development issues in Africa or who want to understand the dynamics of development assistance. Program managers, advocates and grassroots organizers will also find the book very useful. For Africans in the Diaspora, whether in North America, Latin America, the Caribbean, Europe or Asia, this book should serve as an inspiration and a pointer to what each individual can do to provide sustainable development assistance in Africa.

Mohammad Akhter, M.D., M.P.H
President and Chief Executive Officer
InterAction,
Washington, DC

INTRODUCTION

Sixteen selected essays cannot say very much about the situation of Africa, its prospects and its problems. Indeed, sixteen thick volumes would not be enough. In the essays in this book, based on articles I have written in the past few years, I have merely been able to touch on just a few topics in the current situation of a continent of 800 million people. The development needs of Africa are quite comprehensive. No single volume can do justice to the complexities and interplay of forces that have, and, continue to shape Africa's development.

Many other Africans and Africanists have contributed their own writings on Africa's situation, and to any reader who asks me, "Why didn't you write about...?" I reply, there are other writers who have dealt with that topic, whatever it is. Indeed, Africa does not suffer from a lack of written material full of good ideas about the continent's development needs. Many others besides me have been urging necessary steps, as I do in these essays, to solve Africa's problems.

"Problems" - that, unfortunately, is what comes to mind when Africa is mentioned. It is most regrettable that the continent has become known to the rest of the world as a problem place. But it is not without cause. Yes, plenty of writing about Africa in the West shows ignorance and bias. For example, very few detailed discussion about Africa include a discussion on the effect of slavery. Millions of able-bodied men and women and children left the familiar surroundings of their communities and the comfort of continental shores against their will for a life of servitude in distant lands, never to return again or even know their native lands. But strip away that, and you still have a continent with too many civil wars, too much misgovernment, too many famines, a too rapid spread of HIV/AIDS, and far too much poverty. Juxtaposed with this scenario is the continued international development assistance that remains crucial to the solvency of some of the poorest nations in Africa, These western-dominated international development assistance programs make it possible for many poor school children to go school or receive rudimentary health services. In another contradiction, global corporations make mouth-watering profits in Africa while individuals and communities sink deeper into intractable poverty.

As an African who grew up in the continent and is now living in the USA, I have been particularly concerned to see that Western countries understand Africa's problems properly and are convinced of the need to contribute to their solution. For they must contribute to that, even though the main responsibility - it cannot be said too often - lies with Africans. So in Part I of this book, "Africa and the West: Beyond the Rhetoric of Development", I deal with the role of rich Western countries, members of the Group of Eight (G8) in particular, and how they can help to "make poverty history" - to repeat the slogan coined by *non government organizations* (NGOs) in 2005 in their great campaign to put pressure on that year's G8 summit, held in Scotland. I stress the three needs highlighted during that campaign and at the summit itself: for more development, for real easing of the debt burden, and for an end to Western subsidies and other measures which distort world trade to the detriment of Africa and other developing regions. This last is a very important matter which, at the time of writing, is still a complicated and delicate issue before the World Trade Organization (WTO).

In Part I, I also deal with the role of the World Bank under its new President, Paul Wolfowitz, and with the implications for Africa of the possible reforms to the United Nations. I turn my attention also - with two colleagues - to the role of the United States, which we urge to keep in mind Africa's needs for debt relief, more trade outlets, and more help to deal with AIDS, among other needs, in the midst of Washington's major focus on the Middle East and the war on terrorism.

Also in Part I, I encourage closer cooperation between Africa, under the leadership of the African Union, and the Diaspora. The African Americans, Africans in Canada and South America and Caribbean of African descent include thousands of people with qualifications and skills that could make a difference to the ancestral continent. So also do the newer communities of Africans in the United States and Europe - the "New Diaspora" - who now number several million.

From those communities, and others in the West, steady day-to-day cooperation with Africa is needed, not just spontaneous responses to particular disasters that hit the headlines. I include an essay on the response in the West to the Asian tsunami disaster of December 26, 2004; the generous response of the Western public was admirable, but it must not be forgotten that starvation and AIDS in Africa kill slowly far more people than the tsunami killed quickly.

Westerners must not suppose - it is easy for them to slip into doing so - that Africans do nothing to help themselves. When starvation hit the Niger Republic in 2005 help was sent from the West - but also from neighboring Nigeria. For the longer term, African governments have realized that inter-state cooperation and economic integration are essential to improve the continent's situation.

So in Part II of this book, "Africa's Homegrown Development Initiatives", I examine the efforts being made in that direction. There is, first of all, the New Partnership for Africa's Development (NEPAD), the name given by African leaders to a new economic cooperation program with many aspects; while welcoming this initiative, I ask how it is to be given practical effect and urge that it must be seen to make a difference for the deprived hundreds of millions of Africans. How, I ask, does NEPAD translate into dividends in rural areas and shanties in urban centers?

Then there are moves to go beyond cooperation to actual economic integration, for example in West Africa with ECOWAS (the Economic Community of West African States) and Southern Africa with the SADC (the Southern African Development Community). These moves toward integration, on which the concept of the African Union is based, have been slow so far but could bring many benefits. In my work with the Africa Development Bank, I learn about the incredible potential of the organization to reshape the poverty landscape in the continent.

But while they are moving toward cooperation with each other, African states still have many unresolved internal problems, which in some cases have led to civil war.

In Part III, "Africa's Leadership Issues," I look at a few examples. I make no apology for including two quite lengthy essays on Nigeria. Not only is it my homeland, it also has a quarter of the population of sub-Saharan Africa, and its problems are of importance and relevance for the whole continent.

My essays on Nigeria, deal first with the Niger Delta crisis and then with the extraordinary potentials of Nigeria if it can overcome certain pitfalls. At the intersection of the two essays on Nigeria is the need for free and fair elections. In Nigeria, as in many African countries, holding contested elections is not enough to establish true democracy. Genuine elections in many parts of Africa remain a mirage as powerful people fail to provide electoral level playing field for opposition political parties and the civil society. The majesty of the ballot box eludes many disaffected and disenfranchised communities, depriving them of the right to choose their own leaders. Nigeria's future depends on political stability that remains rooted in representative government. The Niger Delta crisis cries out for robust representation, resolution of political grievances and a concerted effort to end the abject poverty and neglect of its people. The people of the Niger Delta remain very poor although the region produces more than 90 percent of Nigeria's oil wealth.

Unfortunately the hopes I and a colleague expressed in 2001 for an improvement in the Niger Delta situation were not realized. We had concluded that a genuine tripartite partnership between the national government, oil companies active in the area and communities where oil extraction takes place should minimize tensions in the Niger Delta and provide employment and wealth generating opportunities for restive youth in the area. This crisis has in fact escalated and remains far from being resolved. While it involves ethnic feuding - the aspect which has hit the world's headlines - it is above all a problem of "resource control": who distributes the wealth from a country's natural resources, how, and for whose benefit? It is also about accountability and judicious use of national resources at local, state and national levels of governments. These questions extend beyond Nigeria, and especially to other oil-rich countries in the continent. The same skewed development which has led some Nigerians to call oil a curse rather than a blessing has occurred in Angola, creating a similar gap between a wealthy ruling class and a majority on the breadline. The same is happening in Equatorial Guinea. When Africans hear that the continent will be a source of increasing supply of oil to the United States and other Western countries, as an alternative to the Middle East, should they be excited or worried, if they happen to live in countries with oil?

The Kenya elections of 2002 showed that formidable African political strong men can sometimes lose. My essay on this election was written to celebrate that victory. Events since then have shown that major problems such as rampant corruption have not disappeared under President Kibaki. In fact, critics of the government charge that corruption is on the upswing in Kenya since the historic 2002 election. But of course such problems cannot be overcome quickly. Every victory for democracy and proper government must be followed up energetically under the watchful eyes of citizens.

I wrote the essay on Liberia in Part III shortly before President Charles Taylor resigned and went into exile and the second civil war came to an end. Since then a massive UN presence has helped the country start a slow process of recovery, and elections have been held - leading to the first ever woman head of state being elected to power in Africa. Despite these promising developments, I still retain the fear I expressed, that things could go bad again in Liberia. The deals patched up to end Africa's civil wars may prove lasting - as has happened, fortunately, in Mozambique - but there are enough dangers of breakdown for the AU and others to remain engaged in the various peace processes for some time to come. In the Democratic Republic of Congo, at the time of writing it is still not possible to say that the peace deal is working properly.

Africa's longest civil war, the North-South war in Sudan which lasted 38 years in all, was at last ended by a peace agreement at the end of 2004. But already, before then, a second civil war had broken out in the same country, between the central government of Sudan and insurgents in the province of Darfur. I conclude Part III with two essays on the Darfur crisis. In my view this crisis poses a major challenge to the African Union and its member states. For it is quite clear that the central government bears major responsibility for the massive killing of Black African people in Darfur, with hundreds of thousands of others being driven from their homes. It is clearly "ethnic cleansing" and may well be classifiable as genocide. No wonder that many commentators have been asking what has been learned from the Rwanda genocide of 1994, which occurred as African and Western states alike, and the UN, failed to act in a timely manner.

The AU is supposed to have broken away from the former Organization of African Unity's concern with upholding the power of governments in power at all costs. Indeed there have been words uttered which indicate that the old sacred principle of "non-interference in internal affairs" is no longer so sacred now. But in Sudan, those words must be matched by deeds. Are African states ready to condemn and oppose outright the murderous actions of an African government, and to act to end the crimes and have their authors brought to justice? If not, why not? In my view Darfur is a case demanding such action. And it is primarily the duty of Africa, rather than the West, to intervene to save Africans' lives.

Wars are an additional burden and inimical to development progress in Africa. But even if peace prevails over the whole continent, there will still be crying needs. I hope that these essays will help encourage both Africans and others to devote their attention to meeting those needs.

Unlike those who see despair in Africa, I see a continent with tremendous potential. I also see a continent that can overcome its predicament. African leaders and peoples must lead a comprehensive renaissance effort in the continent. Africans need to put their house in order, maximizing the potentials of its people, experts and international partners. African countries and their international partners need to be frank with each other, vigorously tackle development problems, and diligently work toward a continent where today's youth can achieve their full potential.

PART I

AFRICA AND THE WEST: BEYOND THE RHETORIC OF DEVELOPMENT

CHAPTER 1

THE GROUP OF 8 AND AFRICA PARTNERSHIP FOR DEVELOPMENT: FOUR ESSENTIAL ELEMENTS

(June, 2005)

As the Group of 8 nations prepare for the annual July 2005 Summit in Scotland, the dire development needs of Africa will again come into sharp focus. A recent report on development issues worldwide by the United Nations concludes that Africa is neither on course to meet goals of halving poverty rates by 2015 nor moving significantly to improve access to potable water and basic sanitation. Prime Minister Tony Blair of Britain will host the annual meeting and his government will assume the presidency of the Group of 8 nations until the next annual meeting. The British government is already off the gates with a major report on development assistance in Africa.

To avoid the rhetorical flair of past annual meetings and achieve concrete, verifiable consensus on how best rich nations can assist Africa overcome widespread poverty, I discuss the critical, essential elements of a reinvigorated partnership for development between the Group of 8 and Africa.

Background

Africa through its New Partnership for Africa's Development (NEPAD) has articulated major areas of specific development assistance. These areas include urgent debt relief; significant resources for infrastructure development; sustained financial outlays so that Africa can meet the United Nations Millennium Development Goals of halving poverty rates by 2015; and the end of trade distortions and agricultural subsidies by rich nations so that

Africa can trade its way out of poverty through better access to lucrative Western markets.

The Group of 8 in the last few annual meetings has emphasized the need for assistance in the areas of communicable diseases control, especially HIV/AIDS, the need for verifiable progress in governance and evidence of government-wide crackdown on corruption. As part of Britain's plan for its presidency of the European Union and presidency of the Group of 8, Tony Blair's Commission on Africa produced a recent report on what the rich nations can do to assist Africa. The British government followed up the report with a four point proposal for Africa's development by rich nations including 100 percent debt relief for the poorest African nations, with savings set aside for health and education programs; doubling of official aid by rich nations by 2015; phased withdrawal of agricultural subsidies and end of trade distortions that make it more difficult for Africa's goods and services to reach the West; and the creation of a new global economic program known as the International Financing Facility that will initially raise funds for age-appropriate immunizations for all children in Africa.

What are the critical elements of a renewed partnership between the Group of 8 and Africa?

Frank, Honest Relationship

First, Group of 8 and African leaders must be very frank and honest with each other regarding what each partner can bring to the table. For example, Group of 8 nations must be very specific regarding their program for debt relief, including specific timelines for the completion of 100 percent debt relief for specific countries. African governments must state clear specific, verifiable outcome measures of its governance and anti-corruption programs. Without significant progress on debt relief and governance reforms, it would be difficult to envisage a robust, fruitful Group of 8/Africa partnership in the near future.

Ancillary to frankness and honesty in the partnership is the need to manage undue expectations. It is unwise to expect political leaders in the West with an eye on the next competitive domestic election to dramatically increase financial outlays for overseas development assistance when domestic needs deserve urgent

20

attention. It is also unrealistic to expect African governments to wipe out deep-rooted corruption in short order without a resort to undemocratic practices and tendencies. However, to provide assistance to more than 300 million Africans who live in extreme poverty, surviving on less than one dollar a day, Group of 8 nations at the July 2005 Summit have an urgent obligation to provide immediate, 100 percent debt relief for the poorest nations in Africa. Poor African nations should not have to choose between debt servicing and saving the lives of their citizens.

Institutionalizing the Partnership

Second, the Group of 8/Africa partnership should move beyond personalization of political leaders to the institutionalization of long-term shared goals, objectives and expected outcomes. It is now a favorite sport to search for "sympathetic leaders" in the West that can "support" development assistance to Africa. Western political leaders know they will be in the good graces of development activists if they visit the continent or visit more often. African leaders trumpet their "closeness" and "rapport" with Western leaders as a democracy dividend to their citizens, even when economic conditions are not improving. The ability to hold 30 to 45 minute meetings with Western leaders is highly prized by current and future political leaders in Africa.

It is critical to translate the Group of 8/Africa partnership into lasting legacies on the ground in Africa.

These are some important institutionalization steps that can be taken:

♦ Group of 8 and African leaders should agree on specific development assistance programs and initiatives in Africa, including year-by-year activities.
♦ Group of 8 nations and African leaders should specify in a transparent way the expectations of each partner. This information should be available to all stakeholders in development assistance for Africa, including the civil society.

21

♦ The Group of 8 should be specific on its level of financial assistance to Africa and for what purposes. It is also critical to set a verifiable timeline on when these resources will be made available and how it will reach intended target destinations in Africa.

♦ African leaders should be specific on how they will create enabling environments for Group of 8 development assistance in the continent, including verifiable action steps and timelines.

♦ At the July 2005 Group of 8 Summit the vehicle or platform for implementing Group of 8/Africa programs and initiatives should be announced.

♦ A major weakness of current Group of 8/Africa dialogue is the lack of clarity on how approved programs and initiatives will be implemented. There are important candidates that can serve as the implementation platforms for Group of 8/Africa programs and initiatives. Africans will likely press for greater involvement of the African Development Bank and NEPAD, two important regional institutions. The Group of 8 is likely to focus on World Bank or bilateral development organizations. The key is to reach a quick decision on the best platform for channelling resources for Africa's development as part of the Group of 8/Africa partnership.

♦ A durable, institutionalized Group of 8/Africa partnership will replace the current ad hoc meetings and consultations between Group of 8 permanent representatives of political leaders and the leaders of the African Union/NEPAD. It would also minimize the potential for duplication of programs and wastage of scarce resource when competing bilateral organizations descend on recipient countries.

Focus on Visible Dividends of the Partnership

Third, Group of 8 political leaders and their African counterparts need to show visible, verifiable dividends of the partnership. A Group of 8 funded and completed highway from Casablanca in Morocco to Cape Town in South Africa will be a dramatic way of showing dividends of the partnership compared to intellectual discussions about "progress" in governance reforms. A Great Lakes region hydroelectric power project will be noticed by ordinary citizens of benefiting countries as they enjoy better and constant electricity supply. Enrolling all African children into primary and secondary school within the next three years will be a powerful short term as well long term testament of the Group of 8/Africa partnership. A comprehensive social program that guarantees all AIDS orphans uninterrupted primary and secondary education and quality primary healthcare services will not only provide a brighter future for the affected children but will also be a showcase of Group of 8/Africa relations.

Mobilizing African Professionals Living in the West

Fourth, African professionals living in the West should become a centerpiece of the Group of 8/Africa partnership. These professionals continue to maintain familial, economic and social ties with their native lands. African professionals are likely to jump at any structured opportunity for them to support development initiatives in their native lands and the continent.

A major obstacle to accelerating Africa's development is the growing human resource capacity crisis in Africa. This is particularly acute in the healthcare sector as thousands of doctors and nurses leave the continent to seek career fulfillment and greener pastures in the West. Other highly trained professionals in other disciplines such as engineering, computer science and life sciences also leave for better opportunities in the West.

A Group of 8/Africa program that guarantees the salary of Western based African professionals if they work in Africa for a defined period of time in a defined target population and for a defined objective can quickly provide skilled manpower to underserved areas in the continent. The key is to minimize bureaucratic costs and smooth out the logistics of paying the salary of an African professional from the West who is now working for a defined period of time in Africa. The ultimate objective should be to encourage the volunteer African professional to spend a longer time in Africa and contribute to the continent's development.

Together with my colleagues, we have proposed the need for a volunteer international HIV/AIDS services corps as a possible mechanism for tackling the acute shortage of manpower needed to mount a credible multisectoral response to the epidemic in Africa.

A bold Group of 8/Africa initiative on African professionals will build upon the current individual efforts of various professional groups donating their time and services in various parts of Africa. This proposed initiative will focus on a multidisciplinary professional response to specific needs in specific geographical areas of Africa. It will provide opportunities for African professionals with training in fields as diverse as investment banking and other financial services, power generation and distribution, information technology and telecommunications, design and distribution of clean water supply and highway construction, to address ongoing critical needs in Africa.

Conclusion

A reinvigorated Group of 8/Africa partnership is absolutely essential as African leaders and peoples seek to reduce poverty in the continent and tackle other urgent development issues such as HIV/AIDS. It is important for this partnership to become institutionalized with specific goals, objectives and verifiable outcomes. It is also crucial to have transparent implementation platforms and mechanisms. Ordinary Africans and taxpayers in the West should be shown visible, verifiable evidence of positive outcomes of a stronger, more durable partnership between the richest nations on earth and Africa.

CHAPTER 2

AFRICA: HOW TO MAKE POVERTY HISTORY

(July, 2005)

The Live8 concert organized in multiple cities across the world on July 2, 2005 will go down in history as a major milestone in organized global efforts to end poverty, especially in Africa. Bob Geldof and his fellow organizers deserve a lot of credit. The focus on raising awareness rather than soliciting for funds was also unique. However, despite the success of Live8, the road ahead for a serious dent in Africa's poverty levels is still perilous. A global effort to make poverty history is not going to be easy despite the genuine concern of celebrities and their millions of fans. How can poverty in Africa become history for more than 300 million Africans who live on less than one dollar a day?

The first credible answer is that the war on poverty must overcome crowd pleasing rhetoric and saber-rattling. There is no magic wand in poverty eradication efforts. Success will require years of diligent hard work, with victories eked out in small bites. More than 40 years of multilateral and bilateral anti-poverty programs show that reducing rates of poverty or ending personal poverty status is not an exact science.

The second response is to think and act long term. Three hundred million Africans living on less than one dollar a day cannot by any stroke of economic or management genius suddenly escape the cold hands of poverty. Social welfare programs of Western countries show that gains are incremental, sometimes intergenerational. These scenarios are in environments where the polity is fairly stable, rule of law is present and most recipients can read at reasonable levels. This scenario is not applicable in many African countries.

Third, the cost of ending poverty is no longer a rate limiting step. Convincing work by the UN Millennium Development Goals project, Jeffrey Sachs and others shows that it is feasible to set aside financial and technical resources, especially from rich Western countries to make poverty history.

Fourth, policy makers in rich countries and poor African countries can dramatically improve the odds of millions of Africans making poverty history. I am yet to see a logical reason why strategies for ending poverty in Africa should be different in Washington, London, Lagos, Nairobi or Johannesburg. If the ultimate goal is to end individual or family poverty in Africa, I do not see why there should be divergent vision on the best way forward in Africa or the West. Unlike the current dichotomous approach of "good" versus "bad" guys in the war on poverty in Africa, the only realistic hope for making a dent in extreme poverty levels in Africa is when Western and African leaders are literally on the same page.

These leaders must be on the same page regarding how to end the choking debt burdens in Africa; how to end all forms of corruption and malfeasance in Africa; how to end trade inequities and agricultural subsidies in Western countries that impoverish African farmers; how to end the lack of genuine elections and democracy in many parts of Africa; how to end extrajudicial forms of justice in Africa; and how to end the use of Western financial centers as the preferred end destination of misappropriated funds from poor Africa countries. Imagine a situation whereby policy makers in the West and Africa reach abiding accord on these issues. The war against poverty in Africa will dramatically change.

Fifth, education is the foundation of sustainable poverty eradication efforts. Free primary and secondary education should be available to all African children as part of any serious anti-poverty initiative in Africa. In particular, African female children should have the opportunity to know how to read and write.

Sixth, anti-poverty eradication programs in Africa must take advantage of the natural entrepreneurial abilities of Africans. Africans like to trade in goods and services, and have done so for centuries. Creating opportunities for Africans to become small-scale business men and women are critical. To make this happen, governments in Africa should create enabling regulatory environments that encourage budding entrepreneurs to push ahead with their ideas and motivate large-scale entrepreneurs and foreign investors to plan for the long-term. An enabling small and medium enterprises (SME) environment will also include investments in infrastructure in the areas of road networks, electricity, telecommunication, water and sanitation. Nurturing a sustainable private sector in Africa should be a major strategic objective of poverty eradication programs in Africa.

Seventh, the challenge of translating international, continental and national anti-poverty programs into verifiable impact at personal and family levels remains daunting. To avoid the scenario whereby earmarks or press conferences on antipoverty effort become more important than actual expenditures on the ground, the most important barometer of success should be measurable at personal, family or household levels. For example, in Zambia, a serious anti-poverty eradication program in Lusaka for individuals living on less than one dollar a day must show trend data that documents the additional numbers of individuals in a defined period that are no longer living in extreme poverty in the city. This is also applicable if the anti-poverty program is for all Zambians.

Finally, present day policy makers can make poverty history for all African newborns. Poverty eradication efforts in Africa should give every newborn a healthy and a fair start in life. To achieve this scenario, every African newborn should benefit from early childhood development programs that lead to age-appropriate and culturally relevant development milestones. These early childhood investments should also include quality health care, cognitive development skills, and, compulsory primary and secondary school education. To make poverty history for Africa's newborn, all policies or programs that are anti-children will have to end. Wars and conflicts in Africa will also end since children pay a terrible price and some become child soldiers. Africa's debt burden will be resolved so that no newborn African enters the world already indebted to financiers and bankers. There should be drastic curtailing of corruption in Africa since children often pay a higher burden as parents lose work and social services break down.

Poverty can become history in Africa if African leaders, their peoples and their Western friends join hands and implement long-term programs that have verifiable impact at individual, family or household level in the continent.

CHAPTER 3

THE WORLD BANK, WOLFOWITZ AND THE FIGHT AGAINST POVERTY

(April, 2005)

The executive directors of the World Bank unanimously approved the appointment of Paul Wolfowitz as the next president of the global development institution. Since President Bush nominated Deputy Secretary of Defense Wolfowitz as the next president of the World Bank, a string of negative reactions and commentaries have arisen opposing the appointment. Some cite his hard line posture in the United States-led war against Iraq and others cite his alleged scant credentials in development assistance. What has been largely ignored or lost in the controversy is whether the World Bank is fulfilling its primary mission to fight poverty and improve the living standards of people in the developing world. A change in the leadership is a rare opportunity to revisit the primary mission of the bank.

If a poor man or woman in a resource-challenged part of the world decides to take specific steps to change his or her status, is the World Bank as presently constituted, with the policies it implements now, a friend or a foe? If a petty trader in Accra or an ambitious shoe shiner in Mexico City decides to expand his business, can any present World Bank initiative or program provide uncomplicated assistance? If a rickshaw operator in Bangkok seeks to expand his business, how relevant are World Bank programs in Thailand to his plans? If a newly widowed housewife in Lima decides to turn her hobby of baking delicious cakes into a small-scale business to earn extra income, can she benefit from World Bank country level initiatives?

In simple language, are World Bank policies and programs relevant to the immediate and long-term needs of poor families in the developing world? Are the present policies and programs of the World Bank geared to smoothen the rough edges of poverty or to assist poor people permanently escape poverty?

A comprehensive response to these posers goes beyond tactics for fighting poverty. It requires a careful review of the current state of development assistance worldwide. In an earlier essay, I posed a series of questions regarding the effectiveness of development assistance. These posers include the real (rather than stated) motivations for development assistance, the apparent mismatch between what the target population expects and what donors intend or are willing to do, and the inherent contradictions between what donor and recipient countries regard as successful outcomes of development assistance programs.

These posers are still relevant as the World Bank appears set to receive a new leader in June 2005. As long as humanity is saddled with the plight of 1.2 billion individuals living in absolute poverty, which according to experts is less than one dollar a day, the World Bank will be a focus of global attention and a lightning rod for social activists.

The situation in Africa is almost desperate. According to World Bank figures, at least 45 percent of Sub-Saharan Africans (314 million people) live in absolute poverty. Recent reports from the United Nations suggest Africa is on course to miss most of the year 2015 numerical targets for development set forth in the UN Millennium Development Goals. For example, Africa is unlikely to halve its current poverty levels by 2015, and highly unlikely to meet the rather modest goal of 50 percent of its population having access to decent water and sanitation services in urban areas.

As Wolfowitz assumes the leadership of the World Bank, he faces critical unresolved issues regarding the relevance of the primary mission of the organization and the appropriateness of current strategies, policies and programs. These unresolved issues include:

(1) Who speaks for the poor?

(2) What are specific, verifiable, independent mechanisms for obtaining the input of the poor in developing countries? A serious response to this question goes beyond the usual "listening tours" or "stakeholder" forums, meetings or consultations.

What do poor people want or need to permanently escape poverty and improve their standard of living? After more than 50 years of development assistance, this question should not even arise. However, if more than 1.2 billion people live in absolute poverty, then either their needs or concerns are not reflected in current anti-poverty programs of the World Bank and other development institutions, or, in the most unlikely scenario, they are unwilling to escape poverty.

(3) Should the World Bank be about poverty alleviation or wealth creation for the poor?

This is a fundamental institutional dilemma. Should the focus of World Bank initiatives be on social programs that help the poor ameliorate the burden of their suffering or should the bank emphasize strategies that permanently graduate the poor out of poverty? A more likely short-term scenario is that the World Bank will continue to support critical social and economic programs in the areas of healthcare, education, human rights and community mobilization.

However, a new president of the bank cannot ignore the long-term advantages of implementing wealth-creating opportunities for the poor. For instance, the best way to assist poor rural women end gender inequities in resource-challenged environments may be to provide uncomplicated, rural-based micro-credit revolving loans to establish new businesses or expand an existing enterprise. In most parts of Africa, millions of African women rise at dawn, often strapping sleepy babies on their backs to head for open markets and roadside petty business centers to sell small quantities of produce and finished goods. These women eke out a living to send their children to school and provide food and modest shelter for their families.

A comprehensive World Bank micro-credit program for these rural women can dramatically expand their petty businesses, earn them more discretionary income, and uplift their economic and social status in the society. Mohammad Yunus's famous Grameen Bank in Bangladesh is well known for its pioneering effort in micro-credits to poor, rural women. Hernando De Soto is promoting a simple idea of converting tiny land holdings of the poor into assets-for-collaterals in private and business transactions. A large-scale implementation of de Soto's proposal with local banks and financial institutions in developing countries can dramatically improve the economic possibilities available to the poor.

(4) Should the World Bank scrap very low interest loans in favor of outright grants to poorest countries? A new president of the World Bank must examine the relevance of very low interest loans to impoverished nations already over-stretched economically by a huge external debt burden and undermined by HIV/AIDS, malaria and tuberculosis. A critical issue is whether the International Development Association, the arm of the bank that provides highly concessional loans and some grants, should become a solely grant-making vehicle for the poorest nations. Since the Bush administration strongly supports grant-making opportunities by the World Bank, this issue is likely to be an early focus of Wolfowitz's presidency.

(5) Can the World Bank successfully manage both macroeconomic policy interventions and infrastructure development in recipient countries? Currently, the bank has extraordinary leverage over the economic policies of most borrowing nations. To ensure repayment of its loans, the bank has wittingly or unwittingly become a major policy making institution for developing countries and a lightning rod to individuals and organizations concerned about national sovereignty, the powers of unelected bureaucrats and the negative effect of tightly controlled fiscal policies on the poor. The new president of the World Bank is very likely to decide whether the institution should focus more on infrastructure development in recipient countries or continue its strong but unpopular influence on the macroeconomic policies of borrower nations.

Another looming headache for the new president is how to assist poor countries dealing with the huge burdens of external debt. The World Bank's Heavily Indebted Policy Initiative (HIPC) for reducing the debt burden of poor nations has a mixed result, even according to World Bank reviews. Critics charge that HIPC is theoretical, rhetorical and hardly at a pace to help poor countries deal with the unsavory choice of either servicing external debt obligations or spending scarce national resources on urgently needed healthcare, education and other social programs.

(6) Should the World Bank become an instrument of the foreign and economic policy of any country? When Wolfowitz becomes the president of the World Bank, he will be scrutinized by non-American shareholders of the bank and an army of the bank's vociferous critics for any sign that he intends to make the institution an instrument of America's foreign policy. A major fallout of the close scrutiny of a Wolfowitz presidency is an accelerated process to reform the governance structures of the bank to accommodate what I predict will be an increasingly assertive stance of the governments of developing nations working in concert with Western civil society organizations. The new president of the World Bank must work a fine line between reconciling the real and powerful global economic and political clout of G-8 nations and the equally powerful moral arguments of a development institution dedicated to fighting poverty and improving living standards in developing nations.

(7) How should the bank interface with civil society organizations? A major preoccupation of the next president of the World Bank is how to manage the often prickly relationship with civil society. Civil society organizations are the livewire of established democracies in the West and the lifeline of oppressed and marginalized populations in impoverished societies. Any global development institution that ignores the reach of civil society operates at its peril. The new president of the World Bank should seek a constructive relationship with civil society especially in the areas of (1) what works in development assistance, (2) lessons learned from the field, (3) scaling up promising programs, (4) constructive feedback on the impact of bank policies on the poor, (5) how to achieve sustainable debt relief, and (6) how to improve governance in recipient countries.

The Wolfowitz presidency of the World Bank comes at a time when the world is increasingly intertwined, with advances in technology and the capacity for social activists to be better organized. His presidency will mark the beginning of an era where opaque decision-making and remote control of global institutions will no longer be fashionable. As an experienced technocrat and a first class academic, Wolfowitz is expected to provide guidance on how best to mesh the extraordinary knowledge base of brilliant World Bank staff members with the urgent, real and practical need to end poverty as we know it. As long as more than 1 billion people live on less than one dollar a day, the World Bank and other multilateral development institutions will continue to come under pressure to reform their policies and better align their programs to meet the needs of the poor.

CHAPTER 4

AFRICA AND THE UNITED NATIONS REFORMS

(August, 2005)

Barring unforeseen circumstances, the United Nations may go through significant reforms that would change its internal operations, strengthen the oversight authority of the Secretary-General, established a focused Human Rights unit and possibly enlarge the permanent, veto-wielding membership of the United Nations Security Council. The critical question is whether these much-anticipated reforms will have a major impact on Africa's development.

♦ Will any of the proposed UN reforms have significant impact on the growing poverty rates in Africa?
♦ Will any of the proposed UN reforms help end ongoing conflicts in Africa?
♦ Will any of the reforms help Africa tackle the scourge of HIV/AIDS and other infectious diseases?
♦ Will any of these reforms help enthrone genuine democracy in Africa?
♦ Will any of these reforms assist African nations deal with governance issues in the continent?

To begin answering these questions, it is important to note that developed and developing countries may have very different motives regarding a reformed United Nations. The United States and Britain would like to see a re-aligned United Nations help spread the doctrine of pre-emption in foreign policy and confer legitimacy to international responses to global threats to lives and property. Russia is likely to look to a United Nations that recognizes the capacity of powerful nations (read Russia) to have deep influence in surrounding states and to fight terrorism in their provinces and spheres of influence. China, as the emerging economic juggernaut, wants unfettered access to oil and gas irrespective of the host nation's political and economic policies.

Japan as the second biggest contributor of UN finances wants a permanent seat in the Security Council not only to reflect its economic muscle but also to checkmate China. Germany as the economic livewire of Europe wants a seat at the Security Council. Powerful developing nations such as India and Brazil with their burgeoning industrial clout and regional prominence want a permanent seat. Nigeria, South Africa and Egypt as regional powers in Africa and prominent leaders of the South group of nations want a seat at the Security Council. These three countries will also want to see far-reaching institutional reforms at the UN headquarters and various UN agencies that have extensive operations in Africa. Other developing countries want a reformed UN that recognizes their life-and-death struggle over poverty and despair and implements policies that have direct impact on target populations.

Poverty in Africa and UN Reforms

It is difficult at this stage of discussions and negotiations to state categorically what will be the impact of UN reforms on poverty alleviation in Africa. It is important to draw a distinction between the UN's role as the evaluators of the Millennium Development Goals (MDGs) and the practical work of fighting poverty in developing countries. The fight against poverty in Africa, for instance, would involve national governments adopting and implementing policies that provide infrastructural backbone for development through network of roads, rural electrification, telecommunication services, quality health services, potable water supply and proper sanitation. It would also require the creation of enabling policy and regulatory environments by African governments, including the rule of law. Poverty alleviation in developing countries will also require significant debt relief by rich nations and multilateral agencies, increasing the role and influence of developing nations in the decision-making apparatus of the

World Bank and IMF, and ending trade distortions and subsidies that block African farmers from reaching Western markets.

Resolving Conflicts in Africa and UN Reforms

The proposal to strengthen the United Nations peacekeeping capacity would have immediate impact in Africa. The situation in Darfur is showing that the UN remains critical to any serious, large scale peacekeeping operations in Africa. Financial, technical and logistic support of reformed UN peacekeeping operations will be critical in actualizing the African Union dream of having a standby force of its own.

HIV/AIDS Remedial Efforts and UN Reforms

I do not believe that there will be any major changes in how the UN system responds to HIV/AIDS and other infectious diseases in Africa because of the proposed reforms. UNAIDS continues to be the pivotal policy and intellectual arm of HIV/AIDS remedial efforts worldwide. The Global Fund to Fight AIDS, TB and Malaria is gradually assuming the leadership role on access to care and the creation of enduring partnerships on the ground. The World Health Organization remains indispensable in developing countries on public health issues, quality assurances and response to epidemics. The World Bank is most likely to gradually shift to grant-funded HIV/AIDS remedial programs in Africa. The role of non-government organizations and private foundations will also grow in HIV/AIDS remedial efforts.

There is a remote chance that if more countries from developing regions of the world become permanent members of the UN Security Council, the UN may expand its current recognition of the nexus between HIV/AIDS and international security to a more robust, dynamic set of policies that mandate richer nations to assist needy nations. However, any expansion of the UN role would be dependent on the next UN Secretary-General. Kofi Annan, the current Secretary General, through sheer force of personality and acute sensitivity to the needs of Africa made HIV/AIDS a major fulcrum of UN operations. It is debatable whether his successor will share similar foresight and personal resolve.

Democracy in Africa and UN Reforms

This is an area where the UN proposed reforms may have lasting impact in Africa. Genuine democracy is still a luxury in many parts of Africa. Organization of elections remains a challenge in many parts of Africa. Opposition parties continue to remain outside the mainstream of the winner-takes-all *modus operandi* in the continent. A reformed UN that can provide comprehensive democracy building mechanisms for developing countries will be crucial in the political evolution of many African states. If the UN can work with African countries to organize free and fair elections in Africa, many problems associated with political stability will gradually disappear. A revitalized UN Commission for Human Rights will focus on practical issues on the ground, helping victims of human rights abuses get justice and preventing future cases by policies that carry legal enforcement muscle.

Governance Reforms in Africa and UN Reforms

A strengthened United Nations bureaucracy with modern technical skill sets in institutional building and statecraft will be very influential in assisting African countries speed up their governance reforms. The key is to harmonize the sometimes over-lapping roles of various agencies in Africa. This will require the UN headquarters to harmonize the activities of various agencies to focus on practical issues on the ground. Technical staff from various agencies such those responsible for development (UNDP), trade (UNCTAD), labor (ILO), gender (UNFPA) and so on will assist African nations tackle governance issues.

Conclusion

The United Nations reforms hold promise for Africa especially in the areas of peace and security, democracy and governance. The chance for Africa to have permanent membership of the exclusive and powerful UN Security Council will be helpful in the politics of international diplomacy. A reformed United Nations with effective African voices will help create the robust and enduring partnership that should exist between Africa and rich nations of the world that control global resources and trade. However, in the final analysis,

Africa's renaissance and development will be home-grown, nurtured and brought to fruition by Africans. A reformed UN can only provide a helping hand.

CHAPTER 5

RE-ENERGIZING UNITED STATES-AFRICA RELATIONS

With George Haley and Sidi Jammeh
(March, 2005)

As President George W. Bush settles down for the last four years of his active political career, the relationship between the United States and Africa is likely to undergo rigorous review and possibly, re-adjustments. If President Bush pursues his stated intention of spreading freedom and genuine democracy around the world, then the relationship between the United States and various developing regions, including Africa, will come into sharp focus.

Current Drivers of United States-Africa Relations

It is not surprising that the United States and African nations have differing priorities regarding key elements of the relationship. As noted by Jonnie Carson, former ambassador to Kenya, United States policy towards Africa remains influenced by its preoccupation with Iraq, Afghanistan, North Korea and the war on terrorism. Policy makers in the United States recognize the growing importance of Africa as a steady source of oil and other extractive minerals. They also recognize the crucial role of Africa as a bulwark against the spread of terrorism. A recent comprehensive article on Africa's "new strategic significance" by the director of an African-based think tank outlined the critical role of Africa in emerging global realignments in politics, trade and international cooperation. The unfolding HIV/AIDS epidemic in Africa is a major source of concern for policy makers in both the United States and Africa. The Bush administration supported the establishment of the Global Fund against AIDS, TB and Malaria to lead a coordinated global assault against diseases worldwide, especially in Africa. The United States government went further to establish the President's Emergency HIV/AIDS initiative to stop AIDS in 15 countries, 12 of them in Africa.

For Africans, debt relief, increased trade with the United States, a sharp increase in development assistance and access to lifesaving HIV/AIDS therapies are critical priorities. Africans need United States assistance to end conflicts in the continent. They also need United States cooperation and collaboration in the drive to increase direct foreign investments, especially in non-extractive sectors such as agriculture and animal husbandry. Africa would also want the United States to use its influence in the G-8 annual meetings to mobilize other rich nations to increase their public and private sector commitments to the continent's flagship economic platform known as the New Partnership for Africa's Development (NEPAD).

The key question is whether these differing priorities and strategic interests will drive a wedge in United States-Africa relations between 2005 and 2009. The appointment of Condoleezza Rice as the new Secretary of State suggests that President Bush may spend some political capital on his twin themes of freedom and democracy, and may push for accelerated democratic reforms in African nations without functioning democracies. This could put United States relations with key African allies without functional democracies, such as Egypt, Algeria and Ethiopia, in a potential collision course. For African leaders, slow progress in mobilizing international support for NEPAD and ending agricultural subsidies may strain United States-Africa relations. It is crucial for a re-energized United States-Africa relationship to have a durable foundation that could stand the test of time.

Re-Energized United States-Africa Relations

The foundation of a renewed United States-Africa relationship should be trust, a clear understanding of mutual benefits, and frankness in resolving outstanding issues and flashpoints. It is critical for the relationship to revolve around a clear delineation of roles and responsibilities for each partner. The Secretary of State will likely reach out to her foreign minister colleagues in Africa. African heads of government and heads of regional institutions are

41

likely to reach out to the president, members of Congress and other policy makers. It is almost a given that United States officials will not shy away from taking a strong, principled stand against nepotism, bad governance and state sponsored brutality and atrocities committed against dissident citizens in Africa. African leaders, especially those who would not seek political office again — such as the presidents of Nigeria and South Africa — are likely to be more assertive in their dealings with President Bush and other high ranking officials, especially on the tripod issues of debt relief, trade liberalization and development assistance.

A re-energized United States-Africa relationship will likely depend on how both parties resolve inevitable flashpoints in the partnership. What are these inevitable flashpoints?

Potential Flashpoints in United States-Africa Relations

(1) United States and African leaders may differ on the best response to the HIV/AIDS emergency in Africa. Africa looks toward the United States for financial and technical assistance in the war against HIV/AIDS. America seeks demonstrable evidence of good governance and prudent management of scarce national and international resources by African nations. Meanwhile, millions of Africans contract HIV or die of AIDS every year. Any delay in addressing the destructive effects of the HIV/AIDS epidemic in Africa will have severe repercussions on the continent's capacity to be a productive partner. In hardest hit countries in Africa, AIDS accounts for the loss of more than one percent of GDP per year. The United Nations agency coordinating the global fight against AIDS (UNAIDS) estimates that at least nine African countries have life expectancy rates that are now less than 40 years, principally because of AIDS. It is critical for African governments to end all governance practices that engender distrust among international donors and development partners. Additionally, the United States must be seen as a long-term partner in Africa's future titanic struggle against HIV/AIDS. United States financial, technical and logistics support for HIV/AIDS remedial efforts in Africa should never be in doubt and should be on a scale that would make a difference.

(2) Disagreements may arise over the concept and application of democracy. As a country built on verifiable democratic traditions, according to President Bush's second term inaugural address, the United States may take a hard stance on dictators and their domestic supporters. African governments will likely be under pressure to implement genuine democracy where every citizen has an inalienable right to participate in nation building and in the political process without discrimination or intimidation. No democracy is perfect, neither the United States nor any other. However, the principle and tradition of democracy are essential to due process, the right to public assembly, the right to economic pursuit within the boundaries of the law, the right to social protection for the sick and disabled, and the right to hold opinions that may run counter to the government in power. Key African states to watch regarding the United States' commitment to democracy will be Algeria, Libya, Egypt, Ethiopia, Uganda and Zimbabwe.

(3) Promotion of transparency and governance reforms in oil producing states of Africa may cause tension in United States-Africa relations. Civil society organizations of oil producing states in Africa are likely to ratchet up their agitation for transparency and governance reforms. Nigerian President Olusegun Obasanjo is waging an uphill battle against official corruption and malfeasance in Nigeria. The geographical area in Nigeria that produces oil, the Niger Delta region, is yet to benefit economically after more than 45 years of oil extraction activities in their communities. Angola, Gabon, Equatorial Guinea, Algeria and Libya are important oil producing states with very limited or non-existent population-based democracies. The unfortunate situation in the Democratic Republic of Congo with its abundant supply of extractive minerals and multiple soldiers of fortune is also a major source of concern. Endemic poverty in oil producing African states can destabilize United States-Africa relations as frustrated citizens increasingly see armed struggle as a viable option. A renewed United States-Africa relationship should pay close attention to the plight of the citizens of oil producing states in Africa.

(4) Unacceptable levels of poverty and stagnant economies in Africa will be a formidable challenge. More than 40 percent of

Africans survive on less than one dollar a day, according to the World Bank.

A revitalized United States-Africa relationship can do a lot to assist Africans living in poverty. Policy makers on both sides should work to:

Reduce poverty in Africa by creating incentives for African farmers to sell their products in the West. Reducing or removing agricultural tariffs in the United States can allow Africa's farmers to export enough products to reverse growing poverty levels in the continent. It is encouraging to note the reported increase in the value of imports from Africa under the Africa Growth and Opportunity Act voted by the United States Congress, with a value of $14 billion in 2003, a rise of more than 55 percent from previous year. A major focus of a renewed United States-Africa relationship is the need to create incentives for Africa to trade its way out of poverty. Experts suggest that raising Africa's share of global trade from the present 2 percent to 3 percent will generate an additional $70 billion a year for Africa, a sum five times the current debt relief and development aid to the continent.

(5) The crushing external debt burden of African countries must be reduced or eliminated. The Economic Commission for Africa, a United Nations agency based in Addis Ababa, estimates that every 80 cents on each dollar that comes into Africa in form of foreign direct investment and development assistance flows right back out of the continent every year, mostly to service existing external debt obligations. A recent review of the World Bank and IMF's Heavily Indebted Poor Countries initiative (HIPC) by the United Nations agency responsible for trade and development (UNCTAD) concluded that the 23 African countries that reached "decision points" on debt relief by the end of 2003 will only have a 40 percent chance of attaining "sustainable" debt levels by 2020. The bottom line is that without comprehensive debt relief, many African nations are unlikely to become positive contributors to the global economy.

There must be accelerated macroeconomic reforms in Africa with emphasis on stable regulatory environment, rule of law, enforcement of contracts, support for small and medium private enterprises, and transparent, equitable privatization programs that create value for the new owners, the government and citizens.

There need to be safety nets for the poor and disabled in Africa. Families that live in endemic poverty have very little in the way of a safety net in Africa. Weak and disabled individuals also receive very little support from the government, including social and legal protection. Savings from accelerated debt relief for Africa should be utilized to meet the social welfare needs of the poor in Africa and create a thriving entrepreneurial middle class.

(6) A revamped United States-Africa relationship is dependent on improved technical and logistical capacity of African states and institutions to implement sound policies and programs. As African leaders seek to improve socioeconomic conditions in the continent, a looming obstacle is in the way: lack of technical and logistic capacity. A recent World Bank report titled *Building State Capacity in Africa: New Approaches, Emerging Lessons* identified massive needs in the continent in the areas of visionary leadership, accountability, capacity building and decentralization. A renewed United States-Africa relationship should focus on specific steps and mechanisms for assisting African institutions and nations to improve their technical and logistic capacities to solve continental problems. A major strategy in this regard could be the development of incentives for African-Americans and African immigrant professionals living in the United States to participate in capacity building projects in Africa.

(7) Conflicts in Africa can implode gains made in United States-Africa partnerships. Africa remains challenged by lingering conflicts in the Great Lakes Region, Sudan, Eritrea/Ethiopia, and Northern Uganda to mention a few places. Lack of aggressive action by the international community and the African Union to end the tragedy in Darfur in western Sudan should be an impetus for close policy and program attention on the best ways to support Africa's peacekeeping capacity. In particular, a revamped United States-Africa cooperation on peace and security should emphasize proactive mechanisms for nipping budding conflicts. This may require greater political flexibility by African governments in dealing with political opponents, implementing economic develop-ment incentives in lieu of armed conflicts, and initiating legal

prosecution of notorious warlords and their high ranking supporters.

(8) United States strategic global interests may change. The September 11, 2001 World Trade Center and Pentagon terrorist attack fundamentally changed the strategic global interest of the United States. A proactive war against terror organizations and their supporters is now critical in United States geopolitical thinking. A major source of concern in future United States-Africa relations is whether the United States may change course. We believe that it is in the best interest of both sides to remain steadfast.

Conclusion

United States-Africa relations for all practical purposes need a jolt in the arm. After more than 40 years of United States relations with sovereign African nations, the continent's development prospect remains troubling. Various development indicators on Africa by the World Bank and the United Nations Development Program (UNDP), and the January 2005 report by the Millennium Development Goals Project of the United Nations, paint a picture of a continent beset with complex social and economic problems. A re-energized United States-Africa partnership should have a long-term focus on issues that improve the lives of ordinary citizens on both sides of the Atlantic. A genuine partnership between the United States and Africa should ultimately evolve into a collaboration of common interests and aspirations.

CHAPTER 6

AFRICA AND ITS DIASPORA: PARTNERSHIP ISSUES

With Sidi Jammeh
(January, 2004)

Introduction

Africa and its people living outside the continent are united through blood ties, cultural affinity and shared history, and to some extent, a common destiny. Since the forced migration of millions of young and able bodied men, women and children of Africa to work in plantations and other early economic activities of the emerging Western frontier in the Western Hemisphere, the quest to establish strong partnerships and linkages between the same people separated by hundreds of years, oceans or environmental circumstances has remained unabated, although with minimal degrees of success.

Today, the quest to renew durable partnerships between Africa and its people in North America, South America, the Caribbean, Europe and other parts of the world is receiving renewed attention for five principal reasons. First, African leaders are now taking specific steps to tackle the economic and social problems of the continent through the reconfiguration of the Organization of African Unity as the African Union (AU) and the implementation of the economic platform known as New Partnership for Africa's Development (NEPAD). Second, after winning legal civil rights protection and experiencing a growing proportion of middle class households in their adopted countries, the African Diaspora are now moving to position themselves as influential political and economic powerbrokers in their adopted countries.

Third, the phenomenon of globalization, with its gradual erosion of national or regional economic boundaries and the instant capacity to connect people living thousands of miles apart, is accelerating the quest for connectivity among people of shared lineage and history. Fourth, the decision of African leaders at the African Union meeting in Addis Ababa in February 2003 to eventually recognize the Diaspora as the sixth region of the AU has put a sense of urgency into organized efforts to develop a durable partnership between Africa and its Diaspora. Fifth, the menace of the HIV/AIDS epidemic in Africa and the high rates of infection among African Diaspora members are creating an urgent sense of shared mission to tackle a common, though elusive enemy.

In this article, we attempt to provide an overview of critical issues that should serve as the foundation for a durable partnership between Africa and its Diaspora. In a subsequent article, we will discuss how to build a durable and sustainable partnership between Africa and its Diaspora.

Contextual Issues in the Africa-Diaspora Partnership

Before discussing the critical Africa-Diaspora partnership issues, it is important to put these issues in their proper context. We briefly review the profile of the African Diaspora and the three distinct stages of the evolving relationships between Africa and its people in the Diaspora.

Profile of the African Diaspora

According to the 2000 United States census, there are 34,658,190 African-Americans in the United States. Of the 35 million people that claimed Hispanic heritage in the 2000 US census, at least one third are likely to have African ancestry. Nearly 1.8 million people from the Caribbean lived in the United States in 2000. About 0.6 percent of all people living in United States (1,781,877) identified themselves as Sub-Saharan Africans. Conservatively, in the United States alone, at least 50 million individuals have African ancestry. Most people in the Caribbean and significant proportions of individuals in Latin America have African ancestry. The International Office of Migration (IOM), a United Nations agency, estimates that the African Diaspora population in France is 1,633,142 and another 1.5 million African Diaspora members live in other European countries.

The IOM also provides a picture of an affluent African Diaspora. About 22 percent of African Diasporians are in the teaching, education and research professions; 20 percent in finance, investments and economics; 20 percent in public health; 15 percent in engineering; 9 percent in agriculture; 5 percent in information technology; 5 percent in legal sciences; 3 percent in administration; and 1 percent in natural sciences. The 2000 US census indicates that foreign-born Sub-Saharan Africans (recent immigrants) have the highest proportion of foreign-born individuals of 25 years and over who have bachelors degrees (49.3 percent) compared to people born in Europe (32.9 percent) and in Asia (44.9 percent). At least 38.2 percent of sub-Saharan householders in the US own their own homes. The average median household income of foreign-born households headed by Sub-Saharan Africans was $36,371, according to the 2000 US census. For the period 2000 through 2002, the median household income for African Americans was $29,483 according to the US Census. Home-ownership for African Americans was 48 percent in 2003. Black-owned business in 1997, the latest period for which data is available, employed 718,300 persons and generated US$71 billion in revenues, again according to the US Census.

Remittances by Africans in the Diaspora to their countries of origin are substantial. According to the IOM, Nigerians in the Diaspora remitted US$1.3 billion in 1999, equivalent to 3.71 percent of the country's GDP and 55 percent of overseas development assistance. Remittances from Diasporians that identify Eritrea as their country of origin accounted for 19.68 percent of the country's GDP and a staggering 85.8 percent of the overseas development assistance. It is important to note that these remittances do not include informal transactions that may be higher than data in official records.

Stages in the Africa-Diaspora Relationship

Another crucial contextual element in Africa-Diaspora relationships is a clear understanding of the phases of this intriguing partnership.

According to Howard Jeter, the former US Ambassador to Nigeria, there are three distinct stages of the Africa-Diaspora partnership. The first stage, the survival and freedom stage, chronicles the individual struggles by slaves to win personal and institutional freedom to live a life of respect and dignity while engaging in back-breaking labor in the West. The second stage is the civil rights struggle in the Diaspora and the struggle for political independence from colonial rulers in Africa. The second stage heralded a new era of legal protection for Africans in the Diaspora and the right for indigenous political aspirations of Africans after hundreds of years of colonial rule.

The third stage, and the current stage of the Africa-Diaspora relationship, is the era of organized and institutional cooperation and collaboration. Any attempt to give primacy to the first or second stages of Africa-Diaspora relationships in today's efforts to develop a durable partnership is bound to fail. The first and second stages of the Africa-Diaspora relationship should serve as an inspiration to focus on the hard work needed to organize and institutionalize the mechanics of a durable partnership. This discussion of a durable partnership between Africa and its Diaspora in this article is almost exclusively focused on the current era of organized and institutional cooperation and collaboration.

Partnership Issues in Africa-Diaspora Relationships

The foundation of this partnership is the need to ultimately organize and institutionalize the relationship between Africa and its people in the Diaspora. This effort requires careful planning, diligent review of partnership issues, and concerted efforts to develop structures and mechanisms for implementing joint strategies in Africa and the Diaspora. We briefly present an overview of the partnership issues in Africa-Diaspora relationships.

(1) The African Union should adopt the Africans in the Diaspora as the sixth region of the continental body. This process will legitimize the role of the Diaspora both in their adopted countries and in regards to their potential relationships with other Western nations and African countries.

(2) There should be clear goals, objectives, and action steps for the Africa-Diaspora partnership. The AU as the political organ of

the continent should develop a partnership with Diasporas that focuses on verifiable objectives and deliverables for Africa's development and also provide value-added for Diasporians in their adopted countries. These deliverables should focus on political, economic, legal, social, and cultural issues.

(3) The partnership should create multiple avenues for harnessing the technical skills of Africans in the Diaspora for the development of the continent. Thousands of African-Americans are doctors, dentists, lawyers, and economists, business executives, politicians, and could play decisive role in both short-and-long term measures to accelerate Africa's development.

(4) The Africa-Diaspora partnership should address the HIV/AIDS epidemic in the continent. Since HIV/AIDS is without question the most formidable development challenge in Africa today, it is important to mobilize the technical, political and financial resources of Africans in the Diaspora to fight the epidemic. The US Congressional Black Caucus has been a huge ally in organized advocacy efforts to increase US technical and financial assistance to Africa for AIDS remedial efforts.

(5) The partnership should embrace the tripartite (government, employers and employees) strategic approach to human resources development adopted by the International Labor Organization (ILO). To overcome the challenges of adequate, qualified labor critical in jumpstarting Africa into the 21st century, African governments, employers and employees must reach consensus on how to address the growing shortage of qualified middle and high level workers that are crucial for a nation's political and economic development. The issue of the brain drain should also be tackled under this tripartite approach to ensure that all direct and remote causes of intellectual migration out of Africa are addressed comprehensively. A fact-based needs assessment is a critical component of understanding the human resources situation in Africa, and also crucial to serious attempts to organize and institu-tionalize Africa-Diaspora partnerships. A major target of the human resources development agenda for Africa should be the strengthening of public institutions in the continent, from public safety to legal, healthcare, and economic policy making.

(6) The partnership should focus on wealth creation in Africa rather than poverty reduction. In wealth creation, African governments have the critical responsibility of providing enabling macroeconomic environment for small and medium scale business to prosper, create new jobs, and spawn satellite businesses. The role of the private sector in Africa's development both in the continent and in the Diaspora should be recognized and integrated into the design, implementation, monitoring and evaluation of a durable Africa-Diaspora partnership.

(7) The partnership should strengthen civil society in Africa. To accelerate the process of enthroning strong democratic traditions and ensure community-based development in Africa, the partnership should strengthen the role of civil society as sentinels of democracy and as vocal representatives of the disenfranchised. Civil society should be strengthened in the areas of policy advocacy, community mobilization, microeconomic activities, and gender equity issues.

(8) Peace and security in Africa are crucial for Africa's development and should be a major focus of the partnership. The partnership should focus on proactive efforts to prevent the deadly conflicts of Africa. These proactive efforts should include promoting good governance, ensuring participation by all stakeholders in the political process of a country, and ensuring peaceful transfer of political power.

(9) The partnership should ensure the rule of law in all facets of life in Africa. The perceived lack of equity in the judicial system is a major cause of political unrest and upheavals in Africa. The lack of consistent adjudication procedures in enforcing contracts is a major obstacle to sustained private sector investment in Africa. The Africa-Diaspora partnership should ensure that all African countries within the shortest possible time have a functional judicial system that inspires confidence in their citizens, among friendly external countries, and among potential business partners.

(10) The partnership should pursue joint advocacy strategy in Africa's relationship with the rich countries of the world and multilateral agencies, especially in the areas of debt relief, agricultural subsidies, other trade protectionist policies, access to lifesaving medicines for infectious diseases, increased development

assistance, development of manufacturing capacities, and increased trading opportunities for African entrepreneurs.

The Africa-Diaspora partnership is crucial for accelerating Africa's development and also as an avenue for channeling the creative public and private sector energies of Africans in the Diaspora. It requires diligent efforts by both sides. There will be no quick fixes. It will require organized and institutionalized efforts to make the partnership a reality. In the next article, we discuss possible ways of organizing and institutionalizing an Africa-Diaspora partnership.

CHAPTER 7

AFRICA AND ITS DIASPORA: ORGANIZATIONAL AND INSTITUTIONAL ISSUES

With Sidi Jammeh and Melvin Foote
(March, 2004)

In a previous article, the authors presented an overview of ten partnership issues critical to a successful Africa-Diaspora relationship. These partnership issues include establishing the Diaspora as the sixth region of the African Union; establishing clear goals and priorities; creating multiple avenues for harnessing the talent of the Diaspora in Africa; addressing the HIV/AIDS epidemic; embracing public-private partnerships; focusing on wealth creation rather than poverty alleviation; strengthening the civil society in Africa; promoting peace and security in Africa; ensuring the rule of law; and pursuing joint advocacy on Africa and Diaspora issues in rich countries of the world and among multilateral agencies.

In this article, we discuss the very daunting task of organizing and institutionalizing a durable partnership between Africa and its people in the Diaspora. Melvin Foote, the additional author for this article has spent more than 30 years organizing Africa-Diaspora partnerships in the United States.

Organizing Issues in Africa-Diaspora Partnership

The need to organize a durable partnership between Africa and its people in the Diaspora is so obvious as to warrant little discussion. However, every partnership, even among blood relations, requires a clear raison d'être. Why should a Brazilian-African become interested in South Africa's politics or economy? Why should a Nigerian unemployed university graduate believe that it is in his best interest to nurture a relationship with the Diaspora in the Caribbean? Why should a Senegalese-French citizen pay attention to the status of African-Americans in the United States? Why should a recent immigrant in the United States become involved in Africa-Diaspora partnership issues? Why should an inner city Diaspora family in the United States or Britain show interest in the political reforms in Kenya? These questions are neither rhetorical nor amenable to easy responses. At the core of the organizing issue in Africa-Diaspora partnership is the need to define a clear, unambiguous reason for this relationship.

"Why" Africa-Diaspora Partnership?

We believe it is fundamental for Africa and its Diaspora to agree on why they should work together. What is the value-added that either Africa or the Diaspora brings to the partnership? What are the clear goals and priorities of the partnership? What are the potential pathways for achieving desired goals and objectives? We do not believe the process to agree on mutually beneficial objectives will be easy since each partner has expectations that need to be fulfilled. These expectations exist despite the powerful emotional need for the same people to reconnect and work together.

Africa is likely to expect technical and financial resources from the Diaspora, access to industrialized markets, and assistance in mitigating the effects of the brain drain in Africa. The Diaspora is likely to expect increased business opportunities in Africa, the opportunity to fulfill professional dreams through meeting the needs of the underserved, and the chance to trace familial roots for those who left from unknown shores of Africa hundreds of years ago. The Diaspora is also likely to dream of a powerful united Africa that can become an economic and political juggernaut, comparable to the United States of America and the European Union.

Neither Africa nor the Diaspora can unilaterally impose its own strategies, policies or goals on the other. The Africa-Diaspora partnership will likely lead to realignment of priorities and organizational responsibilities in the African Union as well as forcing the Diaspora to get better organized.

To move the process of identifying common goals and objectives, we propose that the following issues could become useful starting points for rational discussion on Africa-Diaspora partnership:

(1) The need for Africans and the Diaspora to collaborate on accelerated development of Africa and progressive improvements in the economy of Diaspora communities within a specific time frame (15-25 years);

(2) The need for Africans and the Diaspora to build specific, political and economic structures that would benefit Africa and its people in the Diaspora;

(3) The need for collaboration between Africans and the Diaspora to tackle development issues such as HIV/AIDS, governance, universal primary and secondary education, the brain drain, the rule of law, private sector growth, an increased role for civil society in Africa, and increased political and economic progress by Diasporians in their adopted countries;

(4) The need to jumpstart Africa into the information technology age and create career opportunities for Africans and Diasporians.

It is crucial for an Africa-Diaspora partnership to be mutually beneficial. It is unrealistic to expect a partnership where one partner is a designated recipient. Africa and the Diaspora have a lot to give and receive from each other.

"How" to Organize the Africa-Diaspora Partnership

We believe that there are "critical" and "important" partners in the partnership between Africa and the Diaspora. The "critical" partners in this process are (1) the African Union, (2) the Diaspora, and (3) African governments. These critical partners have the dual role of initiators and facilitators of the partnership.

The "important" partners include Western nations, especially those that ran colonies in Africa; the United Nations system and other multilateral agencies which wield enormous influence on Africa's development; Africanists comprising individuals and families of non-African ancestry who have spent many years working and raising families in Africa or serving as African experts in their home countries; the organized private sector, especially global conglomerates with operations in Africa; and specific civil society organizations in the West which continue to toil for better development policies towards Africa in the corridors of power of their home countries.

We briefly discuss the critical partners, since they have the role of initiating the development of a durable Africa-Diaspora partnership.

The African Union is not only a critical partner but also an indispensable player in an Africa-Diaspora partnership. Without the African Union's political blessings, a comprehensive Africa-Diaspora partnership is not likely to be successful. The AU should adopt the Diaspora as the sixth region of the continental body to set the ball rolling on building a durable partnership. This adoption should in principle be subject to the Diaspora organizing itself in such a way as to be accorded formal recognition and participation in AU activities.

To play a critical role in initiating the process for a durable Africa-Diaspora partnership, the AU should have a clear policy on the Diaspora and set firm indicators for making the Diaspora the sixth region of the organization. To meet the enormous responsibilities of being an indispensable player in the Africa-Diaspora partnership, it is likely that the new AU Commission will critically evaluate the OAU-era approach to Diaspora issues, and realign its priorities to meet the present challenge of developing and institutionalizing the Africa-Diaspora partnership. We anticipate that ultimately, the AU's role in the Africa-Diaspora partnership will be to create enabling environments for successful collaboration between Africa and the Diaspora, promote the partnership throughout Africa and the rest of the world, and implement evaluation mechanisms for tracking the activities of the partnership.

The Diaspora will have the daunting task of organizing itself either as one entity or by geographic regions, nations, professional interests and linguistic ties. We anticipate that initially, the Diasporas in the United States, Britain and France will be the first groups to begin discussion on partnership issues with the AU since many organizations in these areas have active relationships with African nations and institutions. However, to move this process forward, we envisage that the AU will begin a formalized process with a small group of Diaspora organizations, expand the dialogue to involve all geographical regions, and then reach consensus on partnership issues with the Diaspora from all regions around themes, professional interests, and specific programs. A major organizing challenge of the Diaspora is to meet the inevitable frameworks and indicators that would be set by AU. These parameters are likely to focus on indicators that provide assurances that the Diaspora is better organized, inclusive, and transparent.

African governments represent the practical reality of the Africa-Diaspora partnership. The Africa-Diaspora partnership is unlikely to come to fruition without the creation of enabling environments in African nations. These enabling environments include the rule of law, the right to political opinion and association, sustained macroeconomic growth, the right to private property, stable policies for private entrepreneurship, and public policies that promote social progress. We anticipate that a major focus of the Africa-Diaspora partnership will be the need for accelerated regional integration in the continent to create economies of scale, facilitate exchange of technical expertise across national boundaries, and nurture multisectoral, multinational initiatives in such financial and labor intensive sectors such as power supply, road networks, and telecommunications.

Regarding "how" to organize the Africa-Diaspora partnership, we envisage a series of steps, some of them simultaneous. First, we expect the African Union to develop a strategy on the Diaspora. Second, we expect the AU to initiate regular dialogue with the Diaspora on partnership issues and how it could become the sixth region of the AU. We anticipate that the Diaspora in the various regions will organize and begin to reach consensus on partnership issues with Africa.

Third, we anticipate that the dialogue on Africa-Diaspora partnership will reach a consensus on EXPECTATIONS, STRATEGIES, PROGRAMS, DELIVERABLES, MONITORING MECHANISMS, and POTENTIAL RESPONSIBILITY CENTERS FOR EACH ADOPTED ACTION STEP. Unlike some romanticized view of the relationship between Africa and the Diaspora, we anticipate a period of intense discussion and negotiations on why the two entities should work together. These discussions and dialogue will likely revolve around ideas and themes for development among the constituencies of both partners. Finally, the ultimate goal of these interactions is to develop a strong institutional framework for the Africa-Diaspora partnership. This framework requires a strong foundation in planning and strategy formulation, a process that had not featured prominently in past efforts to organize Africa-Diaspora partnerships.

"What" are the Organizing Issues in Africa-Diaspora Partnership

We strongly recommend that the envisaged Africa-Diaspora partnership should go through a rigorous planning process that articulates a common vision, a unifying mission, and shared goals and objectives. We believe that Africa and the Diaspora must conduct systematic Strengths, Weaknesses, Opportunities and Threats (SWOT) analyses to determine their needs and value-added to the partnership. We also recommend that during dialogue on partnership issues, participants should conduct futuristic scenario planning regarding the state of the partnership and its constituents, 10, 20, 30 and 50 years from now. This process often serves to temper expectations and provides focus on cost-effective strategies.

A scenario planning approach also has the potential to focus on the logistics of implementing specific or targeted programs, the role of today's youth who are future leaders, and the definition of monitoring and evaluation indicators for tracking progress. We also believe that the role of the Diaspora in NEPAD and other future African conceived and led initiatives, and the role of the "important" partners in Africa's development, will figure prominently in any serious planning process.

At the end of the planning process, the AU-Diaspora partnership should have a common vision, mission, goals and objectives. These shared attributes should be evaluated at regular intervals or in response to emergency situations.

Institutionalizing the Africa-Diaspora Partnership

The ultimate goal of organizing a durable Africa-Diaspora partnership is to institutionalize the relationship through structures that can stand the test of time. The United Nations today is a symbol of international cooperation and collaboration. Despite inevitable hiccoughs, the UN is still a testament of international resolve and action because of careful attention paid to institutional issues by its founders. These institutional issues include the concept of interrelatedness, the role of specialized agencies for specific functions, the concept of collective legality, and the ever-present threat of sanctions for bad behavior. We believe that the AU-Diaspora partnership could eventually metamorphose into an entity that reaffirms the bond and common aspirations of Africa and its people around the world.

We envisage initially the establishment of an AU-Diaspora Commission that will enjoy all rights and privileges of other commissions in the continental organization and will be active in Africa and the Diaspora. Eventually, we believe that the AU-Diaspora Commission will metamorphose into a political and economic institution, lean, progressive and focused on specific objectives of the Africa-Diaspora partnership. In addition, this entity could become a major platform for unleashing the creative energies of both Africans and their brethren in the Diaspora.

Conclusion

Africa and its Diaspora have the major challenge of developing and sustaining a durable partnership. To build a durable partnership, Africa and its Diaspora must reach a consensus on why they should collaborate, where and when they should work together, and how they should manage the process. Although the destinies of Africa and its Diaspora remain united by blood relations and the common struggles for economic and social progress, no serious attempt has been made to determine specific areas of collaboration and partnership. We believe that the time is now ripe for durable Africa-Diaspora partnership anchored on common vision and mission, and shared goals and objectives.

CHAPTER 8

THE ASIA TSUNAMI DISASTER: INTERNATIONAL DEVELOPMENT IMPLICATIONS

(February, 2005)

As the international response to the Asia tsunami disaster gathers momentum, the major focus now is to provide basic health and social services to more than 5 million people the United Nations estimates say are directly or indirectly affected by the tragedy. The sheer magnitude of the tsunami tragedy, including at least 150,000 dead, will have long-term implications for the 12 affected nations. However, the Asia tsunami tragedy has major international development implications as governments, bilateral and multilateral agencies, and the civil society assess their priorities in the coming years. I briefly discuss these implications.

Natural disasters will become fully recognized as a major risk factor in international development. Until December 26, 2004, most development analyses or projections of the social and economic needs of Indonesia are unlikely to have included contingency planning for a major earthquake or tsunami. Indonesia will likely spend the next several decades battling the social and economic consequences of this tragedy. It is important however to note that natural disasters have been costly. According to a recent report by the United Nations Development Program (UNDP), annual economic losses from natural disasters worldwide averaged $75.5 billion in the 1960's. The average annual economic cost was $138.4 billion in the 1970's and $213.9 billion in the 1980's. The cost in the 1990's was $659.9 billion. The challenge is how to integrate disaster preparedness in short and long term development planning.

Global cooperation and collaboration will become stronger. The response to the tsunami disaster is a pointer to how the international community will respond to future natural occurrences. Governments, corporations, non-government organizations, and entertainers are now mobilized to assist the victims of this tragedy. In addition, collaboration on long-term disaster relief is already underway. At the January 2005 World Conference on Disaster Reduction in Kobe, Japan, delegates agreed that the United Nations will coordinate the implementation of a tsunami early warning system for the Indian Ocean. Another agency, the United Nations Human Settlements Program known as UN-Habitat, is launching a financial program that sets aside funds for the long-term reconstruction of tsunami-affected countries.

However, a major challenge looms for international development experts: how to create the same kind of international sense of urgency and commitment for other daily, weekly and monthly "tsunamis" that take the same toll on human lives. As noted by the UNDP Resident Representative in Thailand, Joana Merlin-Scholtes, 11 million children that die every year from hunger, poverty and preventable diseases is equivalent to one Asia-tsunami every five days. AIDS kills 3 million people every year, equivalent to one Asia-tsunami every three weeks. At least half-a-million women die every year during childbirth worldwide, equivalent to one Asia-tsunami every four months.

The United Nations is alive and well. The relevance of an entity like the United Nations became dramatically evident from the first few hours of the tsunami tragedy. Few organizations can boast of a collection of seasoned veterans with wide ranging experience in the multiple needs of disaster victims. The coordination and logistics of the gigantic tsunami relief operation fell by default on the United Nations system. The United Nations also strengthened its reputation by collaborating with corporations and organizations that have more specialized skill sets such as transportation, provision of vast quantities of bottled water and management accountability systems.

Coordination and logistics of international development assistance will likely undergo serious review. The tsunami disaster is showcasing what many development experts who work in the field already know: the need to streamline international development programs to avoid duplication of services and reduce the bureaucratic burden on poor, recipient nations. On-field coordination of relief efforts in tsunami-affected areas continues to be a challenge as various bilateral, multilateral and non governmental organizations rush to assist the needy. Lessons learned from the coordination woes of this early phase of relief response are likely to spur calls for serious review of how develop-ment assistance is managed. A possible outcome of this review is matching skill sets and recognized expertise of organizations with the specific needs of specific populations and specific countries or regions.

Prudent land management and infrastructure development is now a key feature of international development. Most of the affected areas have predominantly poor populations who live in shanty homes and own rickety boats. Many tourism centers and lodgings appear close to the shoreline. Any serious long term rebuilding effort in the tsunami-affected areas must address the issue of prudent land management and the enforcement of strict building codes for residential homes and tourist centers. The days of squatters and overcrowding in the coastal areas of tsunami-affected countries should be over if the horrendous losses of the tragedy are to be avoided in the future.

Tourism planning, management and emergency response is a central development strategy. Poor nations that depend on tourism for significant portions of their foreign exchange should expect greater scrutiny from the international travel industry, the insurance industry, tourists and foreign governments. With thousands of dead foreign tourists yet to be identified in some of the tsunami affected areas, virtually every developed country will demand accountability from tourist destinations regarding security, evacuation planning, emergency and routine medical care and the enforcement of building codes that meet minimum international standards. Tourists are also more likely to be cognizant of earthquake and tsunami prone coastal areas as they plan their travels. Technical assistance programs for the tourism industry will likely include training on disaster management.

Governments of poor countries will continue to face the challenge of meeting the basic needs of their citizens. With the exception of India, which proudly and strategically rejected foreign assistance, other affected countries are likely to depend on foreign assistance for quite some time. A recurring theme in most of the affected areas is the inability of governments to provide accurate baseline data on their people. Governments that are unaware of the numbers of their citizens residing in specific areas of the country are unlikely to meet their basic needs. A looming danger in affected areas, especially Indonesia, is that hundreds of thousands of survivors, after short-term relief assistance, may not have any means of livelihood as they attempt to rebuild their shattered lives. Increasingly, emphasis on anti-poverty initiatives will be matched with relentless focus on how recipient governments manage their resources and meet the needs of their citizens. This focus will go beyond the current constructs about governance reforms.

Rich nations will continue to spend money on international development assistance. The tsunami tragedy rendered moot the ongoing debate on whether rich nations should significantly raise their development assistance to poor nations. It would be difficult for rich nations in the next few years to maintain a zero-sum approach to international assistance in the wake of the significant, immediate needs of tsunami survivors. Although controversy is brewing over the potential of tsunami-giving to offset other forms of assistance, future natural disasters and attendant media coverage will always force the hand of policy makers in the West.

A critical objective of the coming years is to convince rich nations to take a longer view of development assistance. Rich nations should work with poor nations to reduce poverty levels and create opportunities for individuals to reach their full potential. Development experts should craft messages and policy positions that can build stronger constituencies among citizens of rich nations regarding the long-term benefits of sustained international development assistance for poorer nations.

Emergency Public Health is now an established specialty. This tragedy is showcasing the skills of a rare breed of public health experts: emergency public health specialists. These specialists, mostly physicians and epidemiologists, literally work with little or no baseline data as they design rapid health response mechanisms and coordinate the provision of health services, potable water supply and basic sanitation. So far, the World Health Organization is not reporting any major disease outbreaks in tsunami-affected areas. Emergency public health experts, especially with their capacity to make decisions in the field, will become indispensable in the management of future large-scale disasters.

The media are now an indispensable partner in international development. Without the relentless print and electronic media coverage of the Asia tsunami disaster, it would have been difficult to galvanize global attention and response to the tragedy. Personal stories of grief and miraculous survival elicited waves of sympathy worldwide. They may also have convinced policy makers in the West to intensify their response. A fundamental challenge for international development experts is to craft strategies for engaging the print and electronic media in other development tragedies occurring worldwide. The Internet will become increasingly critical as a medium for international development.

The Asia tsunami tragedy united the world in grief. It also led to an extraordinary outpouring of response. The challenge is to sustain global attention on the long-term development needs of tsunami survivors. A more challenging goal should be to engage our global attention on all deadly tsunamis that go unheralded, unheeded and ultimately forgotten.

PART II

AFRICA'S HOME GROWN DEVELOPMENT INITIATIVES

CHAPTER 9

AFRICA AND NEPAD: ARE ALL BASES COVERED?

(April, 2002)

African leaders in 2001 developed the New Partnership for Africa's Development (NEPAD) with the major objective of jumpstarting the continent's development in the 21st Century. NEPAD, African initiated and led, will orchestrate the continent's determined push to achieve a growth rate of 7 percent by 2015 through verifiable commitments to democracy, good governance and economic development. In addition, NEPAD is a vehicle for a re-energized relationship between Africa and the rich nations, principally the G-8 nations. Leaders of G-8 nations will engage African leaders on how to translate NEPAD into a veritable instrument for development during the June 2002 meeting in Canada.

As a touted blueprint for Africa's development, it is important to assess NEPAD regarding the current and future roles of key stakeholders in Africa's development. Is NEPAD, as currently touted, a representative document and instrument for Africa's development? Are all stakeholders in the drivers' seat regarding NEPAD? These questions are important since the donor nations, in their review of NEPAD, will also ponder these questions. I briefly review why it is important to cover all bases, especially stakeholder issues regarding NEPAD:

(1) Who owns NEPAD? This question is relevant since there is a price tag of $64 billion a year to meet commitments outlined in NEPAD. What are the architects of NEPAD prepared to give up (if any) in the quest for massive external assistance? Is there a contingency plan for moving on with NEPAD if the donor countries are not forthcoming with requested resources? This is not clearly

stated in the NEPAD document. The recent divergence of opinion between G-8 nations and many powerful African countries regarding the Zimbabwean election "won" by President Mugabe is an indication of what lies ahead regarding the scope and direction of NEPAD.

(2) Why was NEPAD a top-down evolutionary process? Ideas for NEPAD and its momentum were largely a high level political affair, often at the Heads of State level. The lack of substantial African civil society, academic and professional groups input in NEPAD may be viewed as a weakness in a very ambitious program that seeks to end "business as usual" in Africa.

(3) How will NEPAD be implemented? Although NEPAD is touted as a strategic document, and there are general statements regarding the use of task forces and project teams, any seasoned management and development expert will like to see a reasonable implementation protocol, especially with a price tag of billions of dollars a year.

(4) How will NEPAD mobilize the technical and financial resources of Africa? This is not an idle question since it is no secret that nationals of African nations, including the most resource-challenged, are leading experts in science, development and finance in the West. Donor nations are aware of these experts.

(5) What is the role of Africans living in the Diaspora in NEPAD? Africa's accelerated development will require a substantial and sustained involvement of its brethren in the West. African Americans, Blacks in Europe and Latin America could become critical players in an honest, dedicated effort to move Africa forward. For example, a buy-in of NEPAD by the Congressional Black Caucus in America can translate into action by the executive and legislative branches of government in the United States. In addition, a powerful relationship between Africa and the Caribbean could have multiplier effects in the areas of healthcare, education, social services, and stable democratic traditions.

(6) What is the role of Africanists in NEPAD? Africanists are often dedicated individuals of any nationality and ethnic group who have spent a lifetime of study and service on behalf of Africa. The various institutes and schools of African studies outside of Africa are important resources. Think tanks and advocacy groups

on behalf of Africa represent another source of natural relationship. Peace Corps volunteers, staff of non-government organizations and missionaries are important constituencies.

(7) How does NEPAD specifically address the HIV/AIDS epidemic? It is widely believed that the HIV/AIDS epidemic represents a formidable development challenge to Africa's renaissance. However, stopping AIDS is currently not one of the high profile attention areas of NEPAD.

(8) How will NEPAD address the needs of small-scale entrepreneurs in Africa? At the end of the day, Africa will likely trade, invent, and manage its way out poverty and economic despair rather than continue perpetual dependence on external assistance. Yet the small-scale businessperson, the engine room of the market economy, faces a litany of fatal obstacles in Africa. These obstacles include runaway interest rates, gyrating regulatory policies, onerous tax burdens, and inhospitable political climate. The government remains the largest and "most lucrative" industry in many parts of Africa.

(9) What is the role of multilateral agencies in NEPAD? These agencies have mandates, resources and technical expertise, and are already on the ground. How will NEPAD change the existing dynamics of the relationship between the multilateral agencies and African nations in specific, verifiable terms? For example, how will NEPAD affect the policies of the World Bank and International Monetary Fund regarding debt relief, macroeconomic strategies, and poverty alleviation efforts in Africa?

(10) Finally, how does NEPAD translate into dividends in rural areas and shanties in urban centers? This may become the ultimate challenge of NEPAD. How to positively affect the daily rhythms of the market woman in Freetown, Lagos, Cairo, Mombasa or Soweto? How long will it take for NEPAD to trickle down to the subsistence farmer with a large family to support? How long will it take for NEPAD to assist a brilliant student who may have to end schooling prematurely because of exorbitant school fees? How long will take NEPAD to save the life of a pregnant mother that faces a likely death during childbirth?

Conclusion

NEPAD is a powerful attempt by African leaders to take charge of the continent's destiny. It is also a strong signal to donor nations that it can no longer be business as usual. However, despite the nobility of effort and good intentions, the devil is always in the details, and NEPAD will not be an exception. It may be necessary for African leaders to shore up their bases in what promises to be a difficult but potentially exhilarating journey to self-reliance.

CHAPTER 10

AFRICA, NEPAD, G-8 AND AID FOR DEVELOPMENT: UNRESOLVED QUESTIONS

(June, 2002)

The development plight of Africa and the tensions between donor and recipient countries regarding aid for development will once again take center stage during the G-8 nations meeting in Canada, June 2002. During this meeting, the G-8 nations will engage African leaders on how to meet the financial and technical requirements for a massive, African-inspired and led initiative known as the New Partnership for Development (NEPAD). The NEPAD initiative seeks to reengage the donor community in a mutually beneficial compact that recognizes and respects indigenous initiatives while meeting international requirements for transparency, the rule of law, and democracy. African leaders estimate that for NEPAD to be successful, the continent needs at least $64 billion annually in investments to ensure sustainable growth.

However, the G-8/Africa parley on NEPAD will be conducted in an atmosphere of tensions regarding the relationship between donor and recipient countries on aid for development. The first salvo of this tense relationship was fired at the 2002 Monterrey conference on financing for development. The "Monterrey Consensus" negotiated by the United Nations in advance of the conference resolved "to address the challenges of financing for development around the world, particularly in developing countries. Our goal is to eradicate poverty, achieve sustained economic growth and promote sustainable development as we advance to a fully inclusive and equitable global economic system." The Monterrey Consensus seeks a developing world of sustained debt relief, freer trade, enhanced foreign investments, better

71

mobilized domestic resources, more and better directed foreign aid, and more democratic and efficient governments.

However, the parade of African leaders that took the podium in Monterrey bemoaned the current state of aid for development in Africa. President Obasanjo of Nigeria in his address to the gathering of heads of state and government, ministers, corporate titans and civil society gurus in Monterrey indicated that he is yet to receive a "single cent" from donor countries in Nigeria's quest to ease its debt burden of more than $28 billion. President Mbeki of South Africa in his address appealed for a drastic revision of the International Monetary Fund's Highly Indebted Poor Country (HIPC) Initiative, stating, "Unless we can staunch the outflow of scarce capital from the poorest countries, we will never enable governments in poor countries to marshal the resources to improve on the quality of public services or to address the infrastructure needs."

The donors, principally the United States and European Union, while promising additional $12 billion in aid for development, had tough words on what is expected of developing countries, especially African nations. President Bush in his keynote address in Monterrey stated "For decades, the success of development aid was measured only in the resources spent, not the results achieved. Yet, pouring money into a failed status quo does little to help the poor, and can actually delay the progress of reform." In promising new aid funds, President Bush stated that "these funds will go into a new Millennium Challenge Account, devoted to projects in nations that govern justly, invest in their people and encourage economic freedom."

The Monterrey conference raised unresolved issues regarding aid for development programs, especially in Africa, which the G-8 conference may not address. At the core of these unresolved issues is the nature of the relationship between donor and recipient countries regarding aid for development. These lingering issues are crucial for Africa since critics of aid for development suggest that despite billions of dollars in development assistance, the continent remains mired in poverty. On the other hand, defenders of aid for development in Africa point out that these aid programs have suffered from undue political and economic control by the donors.

Confronting the Tough Choices on Aid for Development

Sooner rather than later, Africa and the donor countries will have to confront tough choices regarding the purpose, scope, and objectives of aid for development. These tough choices revolve around critical questions and issues:

(1) Are Western conditionalities for aid meeting the felt (not perceived) priorities of African nations?

(2) what is more important, meeting donor conditionalities or saving lives and/or improving the quality of life in recipient countries?

(3) Should people living in desperate poverty suffer because their governments are either not performing or meeting donor conditionalities?

(4) Who determines whether a government is efficient and democratic?

(5) What should happen to governments that have subverted the will of their people through sponsorship of political violence, corruption and economic mismanagement?

These questions remain unresolved despite popular rhetoric by donor and recipient nations as I had indicated in previous articles on donor/recipient relationships ("The Growing Influence of Non Governmental Organizations (NGOs) in International Health: Challenges and Opportunities," *Journal of the Royal Society of Health*, April 1998; "Community Participation in International Health: Practical Recommendations for Donor and Recipient Organizations (Special Report)," *Pan American Journal of Public Health*, March 1999).

To begin the process of providing a guideline for responding to these unresolved issues in aid for development, especially as it relates to Africa, I identify five broad-based themes that deserve critical review:

(1) Identification of Need and Setting Aid for Development Priorities

(2) Establishing Measurable Indicators on Aid for Development Programs

(3) Monitoring and Evaluating Aid for Development Programs

(4) Sustaining Aid for Development Programs beyond External Funding Cycles

(5) Assessing the Catalytic Effects of Aid for Development Programs.

For each broad-based theme, I am proposing a series of questions that may allow for a critical review of aid for development programs, in this case for Africa.

Identifying Need and Setting Priorities

Who sets the agenda on aid for development, and why, in (a) donor countries, (b) recipient countries? What are the parameters for reconciling aid priorities of recipient nations with that of donor nations? How are the foreign policy interests of donor countries and recipient nations reconciled in aid for development programs?

Who identifies the development priorities of Africa? Is it the donor nations, multilateral agencies, the Organization for African Unity (OAU), individual African governments or civil society? In recipient countries, who chooses the target population in aid for development programs and why? In both donor and recipient nations, who determines whether identified development priorities are the felt or perceived needs of the target population? In donor countries, who determines/approves the target population in recipient countries and why?

Measurable Indicators in Aid for Development Programs

What are the parameters for identifying the total cost of aid for a specific country in Africa? Should the cost of aid to a specific African country include project costs incurred in donor countries? How should recipient countries cost aid tied to specific charges in donor countries?

Who sets measurable indicators in aid for development programs, and why, in (a) donor countries, (b) recipient countries? What constitutes "success" in aid for development programs? Are the "success" indicators similar in donor and recipient countries, and if not, why? In conflicts regarding "success" indicators between donor and recipient countries, who arbitrates and based on what parameters? What is the role of the target population in recipient countries in designing and evaluating "success" indicators in aid for development programs?

Who sets conditionalities on aid for development programs, and why, in donor countries? What are the relationships between aid conditionalities, the priorities of recipient nation government, and the needs of the target population in recipient countries? What are the triggers that reconcile aid conditionalities with the needs of the target populations? At what threshold will the needs of the target population supercede aid conditionalities? If a recipient country resists aid conditionalities, is it based on verifiable consultations with the target population? If recipient country resists aid conditionalities at a time of great need, who arbitrates and based on what parameters?

Monitoring and Evaluating Indicators for Aid in Development Programs

Who sets the monitoring and evaluation indicators and protocols for aid programs? Are these protocols set to meet legal and political requirements in donor countries or to improve the living conditions of target populations in recipient countries? What is the role of the target community in the design and implementation of monitoring and evaluation indicators and protocols?

Who represents the interests of target communities in Africa? Is it the local government, the national government, civil society organizations, traditional rulers? Can civil society organizations in recipient countries represent the interest of the target community? Who are the monitors and evaluators of aid for development programs, and what interests do they represent?

Sustaining Aid for Development Programs beyond External Funding Cycles

Did the donor and recipient nations agree on the parameters for ending external assistance before the commencement of aid for development programs? What are these parameters? What is the role of the target community in deciding whether an aid program will continue at the end of external funding cycle?

Catalytic Effects of AID for Development Programs

There is a mutual meeting of minds by donors and recipient countries regarding the use of aid for development programs as a springboard to advance the socioeconomic conditions of the target population. However, the devil is in the details. As shown by the structural adjustment policies of the International Monetary Fund and the World Bank in the 80's and early 90's in Africa, donor imposed priorities can heat up the fragile economic systems of African countries and create significant social and political dislocations in countries that adopted these policies.

A consistent soft underbelly of the present aid for development strategies - according to its critics such as Drop the Debt, Jubilee USA Network, Oxfam and Reality of Aid - is the lack of sustained improvements in the socioeconomic conditions of Africans. According to both the World Bank and the UN Economic Commission for Africa, nearly half of all Africans currently live on less than one dollar a day. By 2015, while global poverty levels will reduce to 11 from the current 22 percent, at least 37 percent of Africans will still be living in poverty.

I will briefly pose critical questions on the catalytic effects of aid for development programs in Africa. Some of these questions are already undergoing rigorous review in multilateral agencies, academic institutions, think tanks and policy oriented advocacy organizations.

Economic Effects

What is the cause-and-effect relationship between aid for development and poverty reduction in Africa? What are the parameters of market oriented economies in Africa and who set such parameters? How does aid for development enhance external private investment in Africa? How does aid for development programs spur entrepreneurial activities in Africa? What is the relationship between aid for development and trade in Africa? What is the relationship between aid for development and retention of agricultural subsidies in donor nations? What is the relationship between aid for development and debt repayment in Africa?

Political Effects

What is the relationship between aid for development and the enthronement of democratic traditions in recipient nations? What are the parameters for "governance" in aid for development programs and who set these parameters and why? Who determines the democratic credentials of African governments and based on what parameters?

For autocratic governments in Africa, who determines their fate? Is it the donor nations, the civil society of recipient nation or citizens of that country? Who determines when autocratic governments in Africa are "making progress" in democracy and efficient government, and on the basis of what parameters? What are the triggers for ending aid for development programs in politically volatile recipient countries?

Cultural/Spiritual Issues

What are the direct and indirect consequences of aid for development programs on (a) cultural and (b) spiritual mores of recipient nations? On aid for development initiatives for information, education and communication (IEC) programs, who determines the message, the messengers, and target audiences? In conflicts between the cultural/spiritual mores of a target community and an urgent need for development assistance, what are the parameters for resolving these conflicts?

Environmental Issues

What is the relationship between aid for development and sustainable development in recipient nations? Who sets environmental priorities for recipient nations? Should there be different environmental standards for transnational corporations in donor and recipient countries? What is the role of the target community in the design, implementation, monitoring and evaluation of environmental policies?

Conclusion

The Monterrey conference on financing for Development effectively put the aid for development agenda back in the mainstream of the emerging relationship between donor and recipient countries, including African nations. The 2002 G-8 conference in Canada will mark a major milestone in donor and recipient countries' relationships as African leaders present a concrete proposal on how to move their continent forward in the 21st century. After more than

50 years of development assistance, G-8 leaders and their African counterparts have enough historical evidence to seriously evaluate the relationship between donor and recipient nations. With African leaders now mobilizing around NEPAD, the stage is set for a serious dialogue between donors and Africa on the best way forward regarding aid for development. To meet the UN Millennium Goals for Development in Africa by 2015, the leaders of donor nations and Africa must ask tough questions and look themselves in the eye regarding the best answers.

CHAPTER 11

AFRICA AND REGIONAL INTEGRATION: MOVING FORWARD

(March, 2002)

It is now a common cliché that Africa's struggles to feed its people, educate its children, tend to its sick, and create economic opportunities for its highly resourceful population are blight on the international community, especially those that have benefited immensely from its abundant natural resources. According to Tony Blair, the British Prime Minister, Africa today is a "scar on the conscience of the world." The Africa of today faces multiple challenges, including nearly half of its population living on less than $1 a day, average per capita income now lower than levels known at the end of 1960s, almost half of its countries directly or indirectly affected by conflict, and at least 200 million people remain excluded from healthcare programs. Every three seconds, an African child dies. More than 20 million Africans have died of AIDS.

However, the international community appears poised to work with Africans to tackle the numerous developmental woes in the continent. The G-8 summit coming up in June 2002 in Canada will focus on Africa. The New Partnership for Africa's Development (NEPAD) is a bold attempt by its leaders to tackle the continent's problems and enhance its relationship with external partners. The issue now is how to accelerate Africa's development, with Africans in the drivers' seat. A regional integration approach to development in Africa is now under serious consideration in Africa. The Economic Commission for Africa (ECA) is dedicating its 2002 African Development Forum to regional integration.

Why Regional Integration

According to the Economic Commission for Africa (ECA) and the World Bank, Africa is the most subdivided continent in the world. At least 165 borders divide 51 African countries. The average African country has the same economy of a typical American town of 60,000 persons. In Sub-Saharan Africa, there is one phone line per 200 inhabitants (excluding South Africa); less than one in five Africans use electricity; there are more Internet connections in New York City than in Africa; and only 16 percent of roads are paved. According to both the ECA and the World Bank, a regional integration approach is likely to increase the competitiveness and growth of African economies by improving economies of scale. It is also likely to maximize its integration with the global economy, create strong institutions to tackle regional conflicts, and create an enabling environment for accelerated expansion of business activities. A regional integration approach may also lead to the creation of a strong, institutional capacity to address political problems in the continent.

The African Union (AU), scheduled to take off later this year, represents a bold attempt to manage political problems in the continent. It is important to state that the road to regional integration will have to overcome five important hurdles: the fear or possible loss of sovereignty, especially by small nations in Africa; the potential loss of revenues, including custom duties; the lack of financial resources to create and sustain regional structures and mechanisms; the potential difficulties in managing the wide variation in the socioeconomic development of African nations; and the fear of the unknown regarding economic benefits.

Moving Forward

I propose that regional integration effort in Africa should be a deliberate process, focusing on clear principles and operational guidelines. I will briefly discuss these issues.

Proposed Principles of Regional Integration in Africa

1. The process should be African-led and managed.

2. African intellectuals and practitioners should have a front row seat.

3. African youth, the likely beneficiaries, should have strong input.

4. The process should focus on the "what works" approach.

5. The twin issues of sovereignty and movement of goods across borders should be addressed at the beginning of the process.

6. The technical, managerial, and strategic capacity of existing or proposed regional institutions to solve problems should receive close attention.

Proposed Operational Guidelines for Regional Integration

A. The African Union should become a fulcrum for ideas and creative energies on Africa's renaissance. I hope that the leadership of the African Union will benefit from a close review of the success and failures of the Organization of African Unity (OAU). It is important for the AU to become a magnet for new ideas, attracting the best minds in Africa, and alert to development trends across the globe. The AU should have a balanced focus on political, social and economic issues.

B. There should be clusters of regional integration in the following areas: Banking; Commerce; Agriculture; Health; Legislation; Science; Political Pluralism; Conflict Resolution; Telecommunications; Information Technology; Energy; Transportation; and International Development.

C. Regional Integration activities should promote the linkage of data to informed policy making. It is important to create and sustain a strong knowledge base on the foundation of "what works" in Africa. Research and evaluation protocols should become automatic instruments of regional integration initiatives.

D. Focus on community-based development. A lot of voluntary, non-government development activities in Africa take place in local settings. Any serious regional integration initiative should ultimately have positive effect in local settings where most Africans live.

E. African technical and financial resources should be tapped wherever they may be. Africans emigrants remain an untapped source of creative energies for Africa's renaissance.

F. Relationships with Africans in the Diaspora should be re-energized. African Americans, Caribbean, and Blacks in Europe are important natural resources for Africa's development.

G. A balance should be struck between government statutory functions and unleashing of small-scale businesses across Africa. The private sector in Africa faces tremendous obstacles in Africa to access capital, and to develop long-term growth strategies, because of gyrating regulatory policies. At the barest minimum, governments in Africa should create enabling environments that encourage the emergence and sustainability of small-scale enter-prises.

H. International development should be revamped with focus on debt, trade, and aid. It is important to continue ongoing efforts to significantly reduce the debt burdens of African nations. The coupling of reduced debt payments with verifiable investments in health, education and other social programs should continue. A renewed push for regional integration in Africa should emphasize the need for accelerated reduction of debt payment obligations and/or debt forgiveness by the West and multilateral institutions, especially the World Bank. A regional strategy on improving Africa's share of global trade beyond the current 2 percent level should be a focus of regional integration initiatives. A continuation of current attempts to reduce agricultural subsidies by OECD countries is imperative: the World Bank estimates that OECD countries spend more than $US300 billion a year on agricultural subsidies, roughly equivalent to the entire GDP of Sub-Saharan Africa. Development assistance from the West will likely depend on the consensus reached on NEPAD.

Conclusion

Africa is already moving toward an integrated economic and political approach to development, as evidenced from the impending evolution of the OAU into the African Union, and the launching of NEPAD. However, a great deal of work remains to be done in welding the different political, social, and economic aspirations of more than 50 nations into a strong regional block. Fortunately, Africans and their external partners appear ready to address the development imbalances in the continent. The good thing is that both partners agree that the effort should be African-led and managed.

PART III

LEADERSHIP ISSUES IN AFRICA

CHAPTER 12

NIGER DELTA OF NIGERIA: ISSUES, CHALLENGES AND OPPORTUNITIES FOR EQUITABLE DEVELOPMENT

With Chinedum Ile
(March, 2001)

Introduction

The Niger Delta of Nigeria is a boiling cauldron and a Pandora's Box that has exploded in the past and will likely continue to simmer for many generations until drastic steps are taken by ALL stakeholders to end the current political, economic and environmental impasse in the country's economic basket. The stakeholders include the host communities, the state (local, state, and federal governments), oil and gas companies and other multinationals active in the Niger Delta, the elite of the Niger Delta, the civil society, and the international community. Nobody doubts that the Niger Delta is the real (not proverbial) goose that lays the golden eggs in Nigeria: approximately 90 percent of foreign exchange earnings and 80 percent of federal revenues for the last 20 years come from oil, the so called Bonny "light" oil.

The Niger Delta is believed to hold at least twenty billion barrels of oil reserves. Nigeria pumps 2 million barrels of oil daily from the Niger Delta. Although Nigeria has earned more than $280 billion over the last 30 years from oil exploration, the environment and living conditions of the oil producing communities are a misery tale of unparalleled proportions. For the inhabitants of the oil producing communities, everyday basic activity is a gargantuan struggle.

They cannot drink water because of oil pollution; cannot enjoy gainful employment because their traditional sources of livelihood have been destroyed; cannot hunt because their wildlife is gone; cannot send their children to school or enjoy basic healthcare because of abject poverty; and cannot enjoy basic transportation, electricity and telephone service because of the "Nigerian" factor.

Nigeria's current political experiment will continue to be hounded by the environmental, health and economic morass of Niger Delta. The Niger Delta issue is a complex web of political betrayal at all levels of government (local, state, and federal), endless economic marginalization, and massive environmental insensitivity and neglect. Furthermore, the Niger Delta question is not amenable to quick organizational fixes, political expediency, inflammatory rhetoric or double talk. Niger Delta represents the rot of Nigeria's polity and its chicanery tendencies, and the diabolical machinations of unrepentant elite both from the Niger Delta and in the corridors of power in Lagos/Abuja.

The Niger Delta question also transcends the usual Nigerian pastime of simplistic ethnic jingoism, atavistic political leaderships, cult and personality following, and self-imposed immunity from personal and collective responsibility. The Niger Delta question is very simple: Should Nigerians that occupy the source of our enormous national wealth enjoy an equitable standard of living, pursue economic freedoms with minimal discomfort, and live a healthy life free from avoidable environmental hazards?

We do not believe that any Nigerian or multinational conglomerate can argue otherwise or respond in the negative. Consequently, it is rational to ask the following questions: What went wrong in the Niger Delta since 1956? How and when did it go so wrong? Can anything be done to rectify the wrong and assure that it will never happen again?

The purpose of this paper is to provide a framework for the equitable development of the Niger Delta. We define equitable development as a shared process of managing and conserving the resources in Niger Delta in such a way that it enhances the living conditions of the oil producing communities without endangering the wellbeing of future generations. We discuss the critical issues of the Niger Delta, the current and future challenges, and the inherent opportunities for a comprehensive resolution of the Niger Delta crisis. At the core of our thesis is a central theme: the Niger Delta crisis can only be resolved when all the stakeholders adopt a common strategic vision and mission that focus on sound COMMUNITY-BASED economic, environmental, health and political emancipation of the oil-host communities in the Niger Delta.

We believe that the die is cast for Niger Delta. No present or future government in Nigeria can ever neglect the unjust situation in Niger Delta without major repercussions. We do not believe that the Niger Delta question will be resolved by rhetoric or grandstanding. This problem will require hard-nosed negotiations, strategies, and resolve.

Background

The Niger Delta is one of the largest deltas in the world, probably the third largest on earth. The region is regarded as one of the nine most difficult deltas of the world, comparable to those of the Mekong, the Amazon and the Ganges. It is situated in the central part of southern Nigeria. It lies within latitudes 4 degrees north and 6 degrees north and longitudes 5 degrees east and 8 degrees east. The Niger Delta is a geographical landmark that grew out of the fanning of the River Niger into thousands of square kilometers of swamps, waterways, vast flood plains, mangrove forest areas, and fishing villages.

Geographically, the western limit is the Benin River, while the Cross River is the limit on the east. It is triangular in shape having its apex some twenty km north of Ndoni in Rivers State. It covers an area of about 70,000 square kilometers, and is spread across nine of the thirty-six states of Nigeria. These include Bayelsa, Delta, Rivers, Cross River, Edo, Akwa-Ibom, Ondo, Abia, and Imo states. It is endowed with immense natural resources, particularly crude oil. The process of the formation of the present delta started about 75,000 years ago and over the centuries, accumulation of sedimentary deposits washed down the Rivers Niger and Benue. The present coastal formation consists of a chain of barrier islands interspersed by river estuaries, giving the delta a shape like a bird's foot. The population of the Niger Delta is about 12 million people, and is growing at 3 percent a year. There are more than 20 ethnic groups in the area, with links to the linguistic groups of Ijaw, Edo, Igbo, Ogba, Efik, Ibibio, Anang, Ogoni, and Yoruba. The Ijaws are the largest group, and probably moved to the Delta over 7,000 years ago.

According to the 1998 Niger Delta Environmental Survey, oil production and other industrial activities, population growth, agriculture, logging and fishing, are just some of the factors that have greatly impacted on the evolution of the Niger Delta. However public attention has tended to focus on the appropriation of oil from the region. From the discovery of the first commercially viable oil wells in Oloibiri in 1956 to the present day, the issue of oil production and its effect on the environment has been the source of constant friction between oil companies and their host communities. According to the Shell Petroleum Development Company, most environmental problems related to the oil industry are due to oil spills, gas flaring, dredging of canals and land acquisition for construction of facilities. These oil-related activities have affected agricultural and fishing activities in the host communities, the major economic preoccupation in these areas. Large oil spills, depending on their location, may go undetected for many days or even months with untold damage to the fragile ecology of the Niger Delta. Thus the simple desire of Niger Delta oil producing communities to survive according to their age-old symbiotic relationship with the environment has collided with the federal government/petrobusiness desire to extract oil with minimum fuss and disturbance.

The oil companies/host community tensions have gone through alternating periods of restiveness and relative "peace." However, we trace the change in the oil companies/host relations to a number of very important milestones.

First, the 1978 Land Use Decree unilaterally legitimized the transfer of all minerals, oil and gas in Nigeria to the federal government. This move by the military Obasanjo regime ousted the host communities from legitimate "natural" or "deep" interest in their land and effectively changed the power equation with oil companies;

Secondly, there was the decision of the federal government to directly negotiate terms of oil exploration with multinational companies, leaving host communities as oppressed bystanders. As described by the British Broadcasting Service (BBC), for all intents and purposes, once oil is found in any Niger Delta land, a well can be sunk, a pipeline laid, the taps turned on, and the oil flows on its own pressure to moored barges or refineries with little or no input from the host communities. Consequently, there is no strategic economic interest to build roads or rail lines, train the local workforce or meaningfully engage host communities.

Then there is the disproportionate share of the federal revenue that goes to the federal government in Nigeria. Today, Nigeria, perhaps as a legacy of its military-oriented governments, runs one of the strongest central governments in the world. State and local governments are constantly short of cash and must depend on the operators of the federal government for disbursement of revenues. Agitation from the Niger Delta eventually forced Nigerian leaders to provide special ecology or derivation funds to oil producing areas. However, these "special" disbursements are constantly mired in controversy and political horse trading;

The Nigerian law on compensation for oil spills contains an effective poison pill that bars oil companies from paying compensation for spills due to "sabotage" and "terrorism." In the ingenious Nigerian way of doing things, the oil companies usually determine whether sabotage had occurred, compensation guidelines are not uniform, and no independent arbiter of the cost of damaged properties exists. Affected families who seek redress in the courts must face the unlimited deep pockets of oil companies, the delay tactics of elite lawyers (many of whom come from the host communities) who have cozy relationships with oil companies and government leaders, the range of land speculators/agents, overseers, political/economic enforcers and Nigeria security forces, and a dysfunctional court system. Today, a land "holder" in the Niger Delta seeking justice has little hope of remedial action.

The proportion of oil revenues that filters back to the host communities has dropped from approximately 50 percent in 1960 to 13 percent as stipulated in the 1999 constitution. Even the 13 percent derivation is a subject of intense political disputes between the Federal and Niger Delta state governments. The scramble for scarce resources in the Niger Delta is fierce and sometimes deadly. It has pitted communities against each other, magnified personality conflicts, forced elite and interest groups to move against one another, and fuelled internecine ethnic warfare and mutual destruction.

As second generation (post-oil discovery) Niger Delta dwellers grew up in pervasive poverty, they could not but notice the posh and lush surroundings of the oil companies and their privileged and pampered staff. They also noted how the local boys-made-good community leaders and community elite live in stupendous wealth while paying obligatory "eye service" to the devastating economic and environmental problems of their kith and kin. In addition, they also became wise to the jumpy stance of kill-and-go security forces deployed to oil producing communities. It is also became obvious to the harried inhabitants of the oil producing areas that the oil companies can play "god" by dispensing goodies and community-based projects, running security outfits, dealing with community "rascals" and "saboteurs", and easily summoning the might of Federal security forces. These second generation Niger Delta dwellers are also "eyewitness" to the fate of their kinsmen in government who do "very well" after contributing their "patriotic" quota to national development. It is no secret that many Niger Delta dwellers who served in key positions in the federal government and the oil companies, in the name of the "struggle", became very wealthy on "behalf" of their kinsmen and women. Niger Delta people have served as deputy commander-in-chief of the Nigerian government and the armed forces, service chiefs, and general officers commanding (GOC) key Army, Navy and Air Force commands. They have also served as petroleum ministers, ministers of finance, works and housing, and mines/power, head of the Nigeria National Petroleum Company (NNPC), director of the Department of Petroleum Affairs, members of presidential kitchen cabinets, head of key Federal infrastructure development organizations and and top managers of major oil/gas companies and their subsidiaries.

The outcome of the complicity of many key actors is the utter economic and environmental devastation of the Niger Delta. The lackluster economic performance of the federal government and the unbridled quest for personal petrodollars by many individuals in the *sanctum sanctorum* of power helped create the powerful oil and gas industry in Nigeria. The Shell Petroleum Development Company, with its control of more than 50 percent of the industry, is to all intents and purposes a state-within-a-state. The inability of the federal government to meet its cash calls and other statutory obligations in the joint ventures with the oil and gas companies further eroded its regulatory authority. Nigeria's environmental laws, despite flowery sections on environmental impact assessments, remedial action, and biodiversity maintenance, remain hopelessly unenforceable.

Consequently, the Niger Delta became a Pandora's Box that ultimately burst with organized resistance at community and ethnic levels. The Ogoni 4 and Ogoni 9 incidents that led to the deaths of prominent indigenes after destructive communal clashes in Ogoniland, a major oil producing area, finally ended the yawning response of the international community. The hanging of Ken Saro-Wiwa and his supporters effectively put the Niger Delta struggle under international microscope and subsequently exposed the extraordinary efforts of the federal government and the petrobusiness to maintain a steady flow of oil at all costs. However, the cost has become insurmountable. As the civilian Obasanjo government found out after the bloody 1999 military invasion of Odi, the issue of the Niger Delta can become an international public relations disaster, force major economic investors to become skittish, mobilize civil societies at home and abroad, and put an unwelcome searchlight on military officers. Internecine clashes between host communities and the oil/gas companies have become increasingly violent with loss of lives and destruction of hundreds of millions of dollars worth of equipment and platforms.

For all practical purposes, the genie has gotten out of the bottle. The present democratic government has put the Niger Delta question on the fast track. The Niger Delta Development Corporation (NDDC) is a new entity and player with the major responsibility of accelerating sustained development of oil producing areas. However, past unpleasant experience with federal government superstructures set up to facilitate infrastructure development in the Niger Delta such as the OMPADEC suggest a wait-and-see attitude with the NDDC. Recent statements emanating from the presidency suggesting a tight control of the NDDC machinery may end up stifling badly needed innovative and flexible community-based responses to the dire development needs of the oil producing communities. Powerful Niger Delta legislative committees exist in both arms of the National Assembly. The newly created Federal Ministry of Environment has the Niger Delta as a major brief. Resource control is resonating in many communities of the Niger Delta.

Ten Critical Issues in the Niger Delta

Having provided an overview and background on the Niger Delta, it is necessary to briefly examine the critical issues that have shaped the Niger Delta struggle. These critical issues represent direct and indirect correlates of the violence and repression in the Niger Delta. We also believe that identifying the critical issues will provide a pathway to an eventual long lasting solution to the Niger Delta question.

We have identified the following critical issues, and will briefly discuss each issue:

- Oil spillage;
- Gas flaring;
- Environmental degradation;
- Poor health status;
- Poverty;
- Pipeline explosions;
- Limited government/public sector presence;
- Distrust of the government/petrobusiness alliance
- Lack of basic infrastructure;
- Political marginalization.

Oil Spillage: The issue of spillage is as old as drilling itself. In every area where there is oil exploration, crude oil spills on the surface of the earth and surrounding waters. This kills plants, defertilizes the earth, harms animals, fouls farmlands, and destroys aquatic life. Consequently, farming and fishing industries, the major source of economic sustenance in oil producing areas, have suffered irredeemably from oil exploration. Apart from destroying the delicate ecosystem of the Niger Delta, oil spills destroy natural freshwater reservoirs that serve as sources of drinking water, with potential health hazards. Since oil and gas pipelines crisscross the Niger Delta, it is sometimes difficult to spot spills immediately and take remedial action. However, the most difficult aspect of oil spillage is the recurring battle between oil/gas companies and host communities over the role of "sabotage." As stated earlier, oil/gas companies by law are not obligated to pay compensation for spills from deliberate, destructive acts. Rows over who will clean up oil spills and pay compensation are often at the core of acrimonious relationships between host communities and oil/gas companies. However, one thing is very clear: oil spillage is a fact of life in the oil producing communities with widespread pollution of creeks, rivers, farmlands, and mangrove forests.

Gas Flaring: Nigeria flares more gas than any other nation in the world. At least 75 percent of Nigeria's total gas production is flared and about 95 percent of associated gas, a by-product of crude oil extraction from reservoirs. According to the Nigeria's Department of Petroleum Resources (DPR), between 1998 and 1999, the total volume of gas utilization for industrial and domestic use in Nigeria was approximately 916 million standard cubic meters. However, during the same period, the oil producing companies flared about 1.7 billion standard cubic meters of associated gas. Much of the flared gas is methane, with high warming potentials and potential destructive health hazards. Although Nigeria since 1969 had laws requiring oil-producing companies to utilize the associated gas from their exploration activities, not much has happened in this area. Gas flaring has continued unabated. For the host communities, gas flaring is a cause of acid rain that corrodes metal roofing sheets atop houses, increases soil temperatures, and visibly damages vegetation near the flares. However, there is an ongoing scientific controversy over the link between gas flares and acid rain according to conclusions by independent consultants, the World Bank, and other multilaterals. The Shell Petroleum Development Company contends that the low sulfur dioxide content and nitrous oxide in the gas flares are unlikely to lead to acid rains. However, for the inhabitants of the host community, the acid rain is real with adverse effects on their lives. The Federal government recently "ordered" the oil/gas companies to end gas flaring on or before 2004.

Environmental Degradation: According to the World Bank, there are five great plagues of mankind: war, famine, pestilence, environmental pollution, and death. The Niger Delta is in the throes of becoming an environmental wastebasket. From the oil spills to the round-the-clock gas flares and effluents from industrial wastes, the fragile ecosystem of the Niger Delta is under constant assault. However, it is still a mystery that no comprehensive study of oil exploration in Niger Delta and its effect on the environment exists. The role of population growth, industrialization, and physical development are also important environmental research issues. The Niger Delta Environmental Survey, largely funded by the oil/gas industry, appears to be a response to this need. However, because of the tentative, formative steps of the Survey and the unsettled issue of intellectual and scientific independence, the jury is still out on the long term effectiveness and veracity of its eventual findings. It is safe to say that until the rumblings of the Ogoni people, the issue of environmental degradation was not a central political or economic issue in Nigeria. Although Nigeria has an impressive array of environmental laws, it is no secret that enforcement has been lax.

Apart from the concern for their staff safety, oil companies have been largely clay-footed regarding the safety hazards of oil exploration in host communities. For example, in the oil producing Obagi town of Rivers State, the road that leads into the village is literally the lifeline of the community. The noise of gas flaring and industrial machinery makes it impossible for pedestrians to hear the sound of oncoming traffic. In 1972, an oil company vehicle on the Obagi town road killed the grandmother of one of the authors of this article as she returned from her farm. No representative of the Oil Company attended the funeral or consoled the family. Nor has anything been done to address this safety situation, 29 years later. The digging of burrow pits constitutes danger to the lives of the people. Many individuals have drowned in these pits. Many have fallen into the pits and sustained serious injuries that led, in some cases, to their death. Burrow pits still abound.

Poor Health Status: From a simple perspective, the scarcity of clean drinking water in the water soaked Niger Delta is not only an irony but also a potential health hazard. According to the landmark 1999 Human Rights Watch report on the Niger Delta, an oil producing community reported that 180 people died following a large scale oil spill; spills have made people sick, sometimes having to go into hospital, and fish from contaminated streams sometimes tastes of kerosene (paraffin), suggesting hydrocarbon contamination. It is important to note that the long term effect of hydrocarbons on humans is still evolving, with speculations on carcinogenic consequences. The influx of moneyed oil/gas workers into poor villages and communities in oil producing areas has led to public health tensions over the spread of sexually transmitted diseases and prostitution. Recently, the Mangrove Forest Conservation Society of Nigeria filed a lawsuit in a Port Harcourt High Court accusing the Nigeria Liquefied Natural Gas Company (NLNG) of complicity in the high rate of AIDS in the Bonny Community of Rivers State. Various fact-finding missions to the Niger Delta have documented complaints of increasing ill health among inhabitants of oil producing areas, and shortened lifespan. It is however surprising that data about the comprehensive health status of Niger Delta inhabitants are not available.

Poverty: The destruction of the land and waterways of the Niger Delta Region has denied the people their major source of fishing and farming livelihoods. One of the most visible images of Niger Delta is the distinct worlds that exist: the affluent government/petrobusiness alliance versus the wretched poverty of host communities. The economic strangulation of some oil producing communities is total, with unemployment rates of 80 percent or more. Families in these communities find it difficult to keep their children in school because of limited disposable income. Consequently, intergenerational poverty has become a fact of life in these communities. Access to healthcare is also sporadic, as families have to make gut-wrenching choices between hunger and clinical care. Poverty and the attendant struggle for scarce resources remain a fact of life in Niger Delta.

Pipeline Explosions: The Niger Delta is criss-crossed by approximately 10,000 miles of pipelines. Most of the pipelines were laid more than 30 years ago. Contact between water and steel will eventually result in rust, wear, tear, and leakage of highly inflammable liquids. Since 1999, there have been a series of pipeline explosions, with hundreds of people roasted alive. In most cases, villagers are accused of siphoning oil from pipelines. The central question should be: What will cause a rational human being to risk his or her life for a bucket of gasoline? Perhaps, faced with severe and sustained economic hardship, the pangs of hunger may outweigh the risk of death

Lack of Sustained Government Presence: The oil producing communities lack any meaningful government presence. In most of these communities, any evidence of local, state or federal government presence exists in the fertile imaginations of government spin-doctors and sycophants. However, there is a recurring government presence in Niger Delta: police stations and military patrol units armed to the teeth and ready for "action." For the inhabitants of the oil producing communities that sustain the Nigerian State, basic necessities such as functional schools and hospitals are luxury items. If they dare agitate for these luxuries, the state will "show" them for disturbing the peace.

Lack of Basic Infrastructure: The lack of basic infrastructure in the Niger Delta is perhaps one of the most visible signs of neglect. Electricity, drinkable water, roads, elementary and secondary schools, health centers, and telecommunication system are "not present" in Niger Delta. At the beginning of the present political experiment in May 1999, the oil producing state of Bayelsa was not connected to the national electricity grid. Oil companies have active community-based projects that are promoted with evangelical fervor in media establishments. However, these projects are fewer than expected by the oil producing communities, limited in scope, and sometimes, patronizing. The oil companies appear to have become experts in "tokenism," where token gestures are exaggerated with expectations of veneration. The state (local, state, federal) appears to have become expert in "earmarks" of major projects without any evident "eye mark" of completed projects. The lack of basic infrastructure in Niger Delta is not only outrageous but also wicked.

Distrust of Government and Oil Companies: In developed countries, the most strategic and resilient partnership is the military/industrial complex. However, to survive, the military/industrial complex in developed countries must remain sensitive to the final arbiters of public policy: citizens that vote in democratic elections. In Nigeria, the dominant superstructure is the government/ petrobusiness alliance that acts with impunity. Every Nigerian government, including the present government, brooks no opposition to this unique alliance. This powerful alliance with mutual benefits will do anything humanly possible to prosper. The oil producing communities understand the existence and importance of the alliance, and consequently recognize the state and the oil/gas industry as one and the same. Thus, it is an exercise in futility for the oil/gas industry to distinguish their obligations to host communities from that of the State.

Political Marginalization of the People: The inhabitants of Niger Delta have always agitated for fairer treatment in Nigeria. The Willink Commission was set up by the then colonial government under Sir James W. Robertson in 1959 in response to the Niger Delta question. The findings of this Commission eventually led to the establishment of the Niger Delta Development Board. The mandate of this Board was to focus on the peculiar developmental needs of Niger Delta. From the establishment of the Niger Delta Board in 1962 to its transformation into the Niger Delta Basin Development Authority in 1978, lack of robust funding remained a major drawback. Very little could be achieved in the face of daunting ecological, infrastructural and developmental needs of the Niger Delta. The OMPADEC and the Niger Delta Development Commission (NDDC) are recent attempts by the Federal government to respond to the Niger Delta question. Successive leaders of the Niger Delta have accused the Nigerian polity of political and economic marginalization. The feeling of marginalization is so pervasive that some Niger Delta scholars believe that the non-inclusion of the Niger Delta in Nigeria's national Flag is a strong signal of a state-sanctioned policy of neglect. The state has responded by creating state and local governments, appointing elite people from oil producing areas to top government positions, and rewarding selected indigenes with lucrative contracts and government largesse. The oil/gas industry also responded with juicy contracts to selected elite people from oil producing areas, providing basic infrastructure to select communities, and hiring/promoting sons and daughters of oil producing areas to key positions in the industry. However, as with all short-term political settlements, the bandage simply covers the festering sores, leaving the source of the problem. The vast majority of the inhabitants of oil producing areas have neither benefited from government programs nor enjoyed sustained "philanthropy" from the petrobusiness.

Surprisingly, the managers and strategists of this powerful and wealthy government/petrobusiness alliance failed to recognize or acknowledge the absence of the natural third rail of the alliance: the oil producing communities. For the past 45 years, the Government/ Petrobusiness alliance has ignored its inevitable partner, the oil producing communities, with increasingly unacceptable costs and consequences. The struggle to end the political marginalization of Niger Delta will continue until the recognition and inclusion of oil producing communities as the third rail of the government/ petrobusiness alliance.

Current Challenges for Development in the Niger Delta

To begin our discussion, we will like our readers to carefully review the National Petroleum Policy of Nigeria as announced by the Nigerian National Petroleum Corporation (NNPC). We are reproducing the petroleum policy, verbatim:

> *"Nigeria National Petroleum Policy:*
> *"The broad objectives of the National Petroleum Policy include the following:*

Increasing the oil reserve base in the country through vigorous exploration in as many parts of the country as possible and making adequate fiscal and monetary provision for the achievement of the set objective;

"Judicious exploitation of reserves to ensure long-term benefits;

"Increasing private sector participation (indigenous and foreign) in all aspects of the petroleum industry through attractive fiscal measures;

"Ensuring that petroleum exploration and development activities are conducted with due regards to adequate environmental protection;

"Ensuring peaceful/conducive environment in the domestic oil and gas geographical areas of operation as well as safety of oil facilities;

"Supporting measures to firm up oil prices in the international oil market through membership on international bodies dedicated to these objectives such as Organization of Petroleum Exporting Countries (OPEC) and the African Petroleum Producers Association (APPA);

"Acquiring reasonable market shares for the various types of hydrocarbons and their derivatives;

"Harnessing the natural gas resources, which exist in abundance but which must be rapidly developed to serve our domestic energy needs with the added advantages of more crude oil and refined products being made available for exports;

"Maintenance of domestic self-sufficiency in petroleum products at market-related prices;

"Maximizing benefits derivable from all forms of petroleum, including crude oil, natural gas and other derivatives;

"Encouraging and fostering increased indigenous capability and participation in the petroleum industry, through manpower training, research and technological development as well as encouraging industry;

"The development of an efficient information gathering, storage and management system, for the entire petroleum industry and facilitating access to such information by interested members of the public and private organizations;

"Investing part of the revenue accruing from petroleum in other sectors of the economy such as agriculture, industries and infrastructure in realization of the fact that petroleum is a wasting asset;

"Encouraging the NNPC as the national oil company to operate at a level equivalent to other international corporations engaged in oil and gas activities, utilizing skilled manpower and current technology;

"Gradually phasing out the present joint venture agreement in favor of service contracts between the NNPC and interested foreign and indigenous prospectors; and,

"Continually developing enabling broad policies and guidelines within which NNPC could operate freely to achieve agreed targets."

As is evident from this national petroleum policy that guides all strategic considerations of the Nigerian government in the petrobusiness sector, oil-producing communities are glaringly missing in the document. As is known to any serious observer of governments, every government and its partners operate under strategic principles that guide its implementation programs and actions. As of today, the development of the oil producing communities is NOT A STATED OBJECTIVE of Nigeria's National Petroleum Policy. Thus, the absence of host communities as part of the Government/Petrobusiness alliance is not accidental. No matter what government leaders or captains of the oil/gas industry will say or write about their intentions for the oil producing communities, the deafening silence on Niger Delta's equitable development in the National Petroleum Policy is disquieting and odious.

We believe that Niger Delta face the following challenges:

Political Challenges: The Niger Delta is facing multiple political challenges under the polyglot political arrangement in Nigeria. The first political challenge is how to replace the government/petrobusiness alliance with the Niger Delta/government/petrobusiness alliance. There are divergent strategies for achieving such an alliance. Some Niger Delta dwellers are arguing for outright control of all mineral resources (this requires constitutional amendment). Others believe in militant tactics that will ground all petrobusiness operations, eventually forcing all parties to the negotiating table. Another school of thought argues for outright but fast-forwarded negotiations to become the third rail of the alliance given the current impasse that exists in the Niger Delta. The second political challenge for Niger Delta is how to strengthen its public institutions (local and state governments, federal legislators and civil servants) to better represent its interests in the inevitable political horse-trading tradition of a federal system of government. The third political challenge is how to strengthen democracy at community levels in Niger Delta so that the community leaders will consistently represent their constituent views and interests. The final political challenge is how to hold each Niger Delta inhabitant in a position of authority accountable for his/her actions at all times. A resolution of this fourth challenge will take care of indigenes that take convenient "sabbatical" leave from the Niger Delta struggle during their forays in government and petrobusiness circles. They often come back from such forays wealthier, and ready to lead the struggle for "resource control" in Niger Delta.

Socioeconomic Challenges: A hungry man/woman is an angry person. Many Niger Delta families are both hungry and angry. The daily struggle for "survival" is alive and well in Niger Delta. The first and immediate socioeconomic challenge is to provide public and private sector jobs for the large numbers of unemployed and underemployed individuals. To end the restiveness of youth and young adults in Niger Delta, the issue of personal and community poverty must be addressed. The second challenge is improve the basic infrastructure (electricity, roads, telephones, schools, health centers, and so on) in the Niger Delta so that private enterprise can flourish and quality of life can improve. The third challenge is to improve the educational capacity of young persons in the Niger Delta so as to prepare them for gainful employment.

Environmental Challenges: The Niger Delta topography is by itself challenging. Add the environmental effects of petrobusiness to the mix, and you have the makings of a major environmental disaster. The challenge is multifaceted, onerous, and requires urgent remedial action. The first major environmental challenge is to clean up the pollution from petrobusiness in the Niger Delta. The second challenge is maintain the fragile ecosystem of the Niger Delta through integrated biodiversity management. The third challenge is to reach a consensus on how to maintain the basic livelihoods of oil producing communities (fishing and farming) in the presence of petroleum exploration.

Opportunities for Equitable Development in the Niger Delta

The Niger Delta is a marvel of creation. Its mangrove forests, swamps, numerous tributaries of the River Niger, the unique flora and fauna, the delicate fresh water/brackish water balance, the numerous species of fish, animals, birds and reptiles sustain a delicate ecosystem. The discovery of oil and gas created a crisis situation in the Niger Delta. However, for every crisis, there may be a silver lining. We believe that there are multiple silver linings in the continued saga of Niger Delta that can serve as unique opportunities for sustained, equitable development of the oil producing areas of Nigeria.

First, we believe the current standoff between the government/petrobusiness alliance and the host communities has reached an impasse. There can never be business as usual again in Niger Delta. There is no viable alternative to a Niger Delta/government/petrobusiness alliance. This alliance will change the current power imbalance in Nigeria's oil equation by allowing oil-producing communities (not just selected elite) the opportunity to actively participate in strategic decision making in the areas of oil exploration and compensation, environmental management, community development, and management of resources reserved for Niger Delta. A functional Niger Delta/government/petrobusiness alliance will devote equal attention to petroleum/gas exploration, soil and water conservation, and the prudent management of the environment. The alliance could also become the nexus of an accelerated private sector development in Niger Delta that can provide gainful employment to indigent families. For example, the provision of micro credit facilities to poor families can accelerate the creation of small-scale industries that can sustain families and provide jobs. In addition, the alliance can accelerate research in the following areas: an independent environmental survey of Niger Delta; a population-based health survey of oil producing communities; a scientific study of direct and indirect effects of oil pollution in Niger Delta; and a study of macroeconomic and microeconomic consequences of the loss of livelihood from fishing and farming, the major economic pursuit of oil producing communities.

It is important to state that we see structures such as the NDDC as representing government interests in the proposed alliance. Because of our belief that in a strategic alliance you can never serve two major interests even if they are compatible, we are proposing that there should be a clear separation between the representatives of local/state governments and those of oil-producing communities.

Representatives of oil communities in the alliance will be elected solely for that purpose and should live in these communities. They can coordinate common issues with their kith and kin in local, state, and federal governments. For example, any legislative effort to incorporate the development of the Niger Delta in the National Petroleum Policy will require close collaboration between representatives of oil producing companies and Niger Delta representatives in state and national assemblies. As shown by our model of the Niger Delta/government/petrobusiness alliance, equitable development of the oil producing communities should be the glue that holds the alliance together.

Second, the current political experiment in Nigeria offers a unique opportunity to address the Niger Delta question in a non-military fashion. The political leaders of the Niger Delta are in a unique position to review/revamp existing political alliances as they pursue the logical conclusion of the Niger Delta question.

Third, Niger Delta inhabitants now have the opportunity to do a sincere soul searching among themselves regarding their past and current representatives in the Nigeria polity. Is every Niger Delta son or daughter in the corridors of power and the oil/gas industry doing their best to improve the lot of oil producing communities?

Fourth, the international community is maintaining eternal vigilance on the events in the Niger Delta for both commercial and altruistic reasons. As it is the goose that lays the golden eggs, Western countries are unlikely to tolerate continued unrest and/or high handedness from security agencies in Niger Delta. The powerful civil society organizations in the West, especially the environmental and human rights lobbies are now highly mobilized by the blatant injustices in Niger Delta. Prominent print and electronic media organizations in the West have published and/or broadcast unflattering articles on the activities of the government/petrobusiness alliance in the Niger Delta. Local non-government organizations (NGOs) dealing with various Niger Delta issues have sprung up in the last few years, with formidable legal, research, advocacy, and organizing capacities. Niger Delta organizations in North America and Europe are active in top policy circles of Western governments.

Finally, the restive youths of the Niger Delta have sent strong signals to all policy makers in Nigeria that the era of appeasing the elite of Niger Delta in lieu of a comprehensive community-based development strategy is over. Any future development efforts in the Niger Delta will be assessed by noticeable improvements in the quality of life of families that live in the villages of the Niger Delta.

Conclusion

We believe that the die is cast for the Niger Delta. No present or future government in Nigeria can ever neglect the unjust situation in the Niger Delta without major repercussions. We do not believe that the Niger Delta question will be resolved by rhetoric or grandstanding. This problem will require hard-nosed negotiations, strategies, and resolve. It will require the enthronement of a viable alliance that recognizes the recurring role of the three key stakeholders: the oil-producing communities, the state, and the petrobusiness. It will also require Niger Delta dwellers, especially their elite, to look themselves in the mirror and ask hard questions. Finally, it must be about the men, women and children that have never benefited from the gushing Nigerian petrodollars.

CHAPTER 13

THE PROMISE OF NIGERIA

(October, 2005)

As Nigeria celebrated its 45th day of independence, I could not but reflect on the immense promise of a country chosen and destined for greatness. I am also aware that the great promise of Nigeria is yet to materialize, and many people do not believe that Nigeria will reach its full potential. However, since I became actively involved on African issues especially through the lens of HIV/AIDS remedial efforts and as I became more exposed to the intricacies of global politics, I became aware of the tacit understanding among the comity of nations, especially the most influential nations in the world, on Nigeria's limitless promise. However, what is not limitless is how long other influential nations will wait for Nigeria to get its act together and fulfill its promise.

Why do I think that Nigeria has great promise?

First, the era of atomization of nation states is gradually disappearing. According to the World Bank, the economy of Africa is about the size of Belgium. Most countries in Africa have national economies equivalent to the size of county or district governments in the United States. It is increasingly difficult for countries with very modest economies or landlocked borders to manage the expenses of national and international statecraft and diplomacy. As the most populous nation in Africa, Nigeria by default is looked upon by Western and smaller African nations as a major anchor of stability in the continent. It would be very difficult for Western nations to allow the disintegration of Nigeria. It would also be very difficult for the countries in West Africa or smaller states in Africa through the instrument of the African Union to allow Nigeria to break apart.

Second, Nigeria produces a sizeable proportion of intellectuals and professionals of all persuasions in Africa and in the Black world. Every years, thousands of young men and women graduate from scores of Nigerian universities, polytechnics, colleges of education and technical schools. Today, these graduates may not be gainfully employed because of Nigeria's dire economic straits but they represent a potentially manageable and educated workforce. It is no secret that global conglomerates see Nigeria as the crown jewel of investments in Africa because of its population and its potentially trainable workforce. These unemployed or underemployed educated individuals also have the option of starting their own business enterprises and providing employment opportunities for other individuals. Nigerian newspapers report regularly on these enterprising men and women who moved from walking the streets in search of jobs to starting their own businesses and hiring staff. Furthermore, Nigerian intellectuals living outside the country are growing in numbers, substance and influence. Gradually, some of these intellectuals are gaining policy influence in their adopted or host countries, with the potential capacity to shape Western reaction to events in Nigeria.

Third, Nigeria share of natural resources are extensive. Nigeria, in addition to the well known oil resource is also endowed with solid minerals in various parts of the country. Nigeria also has the capacity to become a major exporter of cassava and sugar. The country can also easily become a major exporter of processed cocoa and groundnuts. Nigeria's vast liquid and solid mineral deposits if properly managed can transform the country into a major force in global economy. It can also unleash the natural entrepreneurial spirit of its citizens. I believe that with the global crackdown on money laundering and the ongoing, unprecedented cooperation among international law enforcement agencies, it would become increasingly difficult to siphon Nigeria's scarce foreign earnings into private accounts or mismanage public funds.

Fourth, Nigeria today has a strong economic team. Whether you agree with their market-orientation philosophy or not, whether you agree with the Paris Club debt relief or not, the economic team led by the Finance Minister, Ngozi Okonjo-Iweala is implementing disciplined micro-and-macro economic policies that on paper will ultimately lead to a scenario whereby the government provides sound enabling environments for private enterprises, enforces the rule of law and contract, and, provides verifiable evaluation benchmarks. Although the Obasanjo government economic policies may unravel when the president leaves office in 2007, it would be very difficult for the next government to radically alter the course of Nigeria's economy.

Fifth, Nigeria's politics will be undergoing major reform before the elections in 2007. For the first time since Nigeria's independence 45 years, there will be three powerful political tendencies that will contend for power in Nigeria. These three tendencies know each other inside-out, have extensive financial and logistics resources and understand the powers and limitations of incumbency. The Obasanjo, Atiku Abubakar and Ibrahim Babangida political groups in Nigeria are likely to neutralize each other in terms of "preparations" for elections. Winning party primaries is simply the beginning of the political musical chairs as "defeated" groups easily regroup, metamorphose or swallow up existing parties in the country. The current political rumbling in Nigeria is directly traceable to pre-election jitters and maneuvers of these powerful political blocks. The unanticipated outcome is that it would be very difficult to brazenly manipulate 2007 elections in Nigeria. Thus, political stability, the albatross of Nigeria's corporate existence, is likely to be assured in a rather bizarre fashion.

Sixth, I am not aware of any serious living Nigerian politician who by instinct or deliberate action is contemplating the break up of Nigeria's territorial integrity and continued corporate existence. Prominent Nigerian political families have now developed Siamese relationships with their counterparts from all over country through marriages, business partnerships, professional association and political affiliations. Despite the occasional, half-hearted cantor to ethnic jingoism, Nigeria politicians by their deliberate actions have shown their continued preference for Nigeria as we know it today.

Seventh, war or Darfur style genocide is unlikely in Nigeria due to a combination of factors. Nigeria barely survived a fratricidal civil war. Another civil war is an unlikely proposition at this point in time. In addition, Nigerian politicians are unlikely to exchange their current lifestyle of pomp and pageantry for that of a drab-yoked guerrilla leader who keeps one eye on his or her piston and another eye on statecraft responsibilities. Nigerian politicians are also unlikely to choose a life of living rough in the bush. Again, unlike the situation during the Nigeria's civil war, major Western powers are likely to nip in the bud any attempt to break up Nigeria or do anything to jeopardize Nigeria's corporate existence. A religious war in Nigeria is also unlikely because in the Northern part of the country with majority Moslem population, Christian minorities have shown in recent communal clashes that they are no pushovers. It is almost inconceivable that Moslems and Christians in the Western part of Nigeria will fight each other over religious differences.

Eight, Nigerians in the Diaspora are gradually waking up to their responsibilities in Nigeria. With a growing level of remittances back home and increasingly being called upon to shoulder responsibilities at family and village level, Nigerians in Diaspora are gradually becoming political and by 2007 many will go home to contest for various offices and campaign vigorously for their candidates. Nigerians in Diaspora are also poised to make their mark through investigative journalism, judicial processes and political action in the United States, United Kingdom and other Western countries to ensure free-and-fair elections in Nigeria and to track down assets of public officials. The influence of Nigerians in the Diaspora will grow irrespective of whether dual citizenship is recognized for voting purposes or not.

Ninth, younger generations of Nigerians that grew up in the urban centers, schooled in various parts of the country and intermarrying outside their ethnic groups, are unlikely to see things purely from tribal perspectives. These Nigerians most of whom were born after the end of the civil war in 1970 have a more global perspective to life, readily recognize the interconnectedness of the global community, and, are inherently suspicious of self proclaimed economic, political or social Messiahs. The so-called MTV generation is also more likely to demand more from their leaders and hold them accountable for their actions while in office.

Tenth, Nigeria and South Africa are extremely important countries in any future plan or renaissance for Africa. The need to seriously address social and economic problems in Africa will have salutary effect on the most populous and the most economically powerful nations in the continent. I see a greater mutually beneficial cooperation between Nigeria and South Africa as the two countries face delicate political transitions in 2007 (Nigeria) and 2009 (South Africa). I also see greater collaboration as the two countries navigate through long term economic flashpoints (controlling high poverty rates in Nigeria and allowing black participation in South Africa's economy).

Conclusion

Nigeria's promise is easily achievable. None of the aforementioned ten points is complicated. However, two critical tests await Nigeria: the 2007 national, state and local elections and the absolute need to know the census figures of Nigeria so that effective planning and policy making could take place. I believe that Nigerians will work very hard to ensure that the country pass these critical tests and set the stage for the giant of Africa to take its right place in the comity of nations.

CHAPTER 14

KENYA'S 2002 ELECTIONS: TEN LESSONS

(January, 2003)

The swift and peaceful transition of power on December 30, 2002 made every Kenyan, African, and lover of peace extremely happy. President Mwai Kibaki and his National Rainbow Coalition (NARC) trounced the ruling party, KANU in the presidential, parliamentary and local elections. The people of Kenya have spoken and their choice heard around the world. The resounding victory of the Opposition over the ruling party has multiple lessons for fledgling democracies around the world, especially in Africa. I briefly discuss ten such lessons.

The era of the big man is over. Ex-President Moi is among the last breed of big men in politics and government in Africa. I do not believe that Moi knew what hit him in this election. Kenyans, like most people everywhere, are now tired of omnipotent leadership. Kenyans decided that it is no longer necessary to catch cold whenever their leader sneezes or to sing a daily lullaby to their leader.

The power of incumbency is overblown. Most Africans know that the power of incumbency in the continent is tied closely to the ability to manipulate and rig elections. Once that route is foreclosed, most incumbent governments in Africa may not survive the majesty of the ballot box. KANU was no exception.

A few people can make a difference. Margaret Mead famously stated that "never doubt that a small group of thoughtful, committed citizens can change the world." The leadership of NARC put their career on the line to challenge a powerful and well-entrenched ruling party. Of all these NARC leaders, Raila Odinga emerges as the hero of the silent and peaceful revolution that swept away the ruling party. By daring to challenge the powerful interests that had ruled Kenya for 39 years and foregoing his own presidential ambition, Raila Odinga has shown that a single individual and a few good men and women can make the impossible dramatically possible.

Wananchi (ordinary people) are no fools. Politicians since independence in the early 1960s in many parts of Africa have perfected a simple approach to governance: play up ethnicity; divide and conquer opposition groups; display paraphernalia of office to bedazzle citizens, and sprinkle token sums of money during elections. *Wananchi* simply said no in Kenya and may have rewritten the play book of African politics. In the parliamentary elections of Kenya, many politicians lost their deposit after spending huge sums of "democracy dividends" on prospective voters, according to press reports. A KANU politician who reportedly completed an electricity project within a month prior to the elections also lost heavily.

Election-only politicians are now in trouble. This election clearly shows that fly-by-the-night politicians are now an endangered species. For every politician in Kenya today, the voters sent a clear message: if we see or hear from you only during electioneering campaigns, we will retire you prematurely.

Tribal jingoists need to go back to the drawing board. This is one of the most important lessons from this election in a society that is heavily tribalized. Ex-vice president Musa Mudavadi lost his parliamentary seat despite the rosy promises of a continued vice presidential slot for his tribe. The choice of Mwai Kibaki by the NARC as the consensus candidate for presidency effectively put paid to the strategic choice of Uhuru Kenyatta, a fellow Kikuyu.

Corruption has finally become a dirty word. KANU over the years became synonymous with corruption, and voters decided that enough is enough. One of the most interesting spectacles during the months leading to the election was the scramble by politicians to abandon the KANU platform. For the first time in my memory, politicians in Africa (here, Kenya) struggled to outdo each other in denouncing corruption and its destructive effects.

Being a stooge or being seen as one is a kiss of political death. Uhuru Kenyatta simply had no chance in the presidential election because he was widely perceived to be a stooge of powerful interests in the former ruling party, KANU. Despite an admirable campaign and valiant denials of not being a stooge, Uhuru could not escape the political coal tar of his backers. The upside to this situation is that every young politician in the future will think twice before accepting to be the "anointed" one in a reviled government.

Citizens can take back their government. The people of Kenya have sent a clear message to the long-suffering masses in many parts of Africa: you can take back your government. The political earthquake in Kenya has revalidated the majesty of the ballot box and reinvigorated the power of political choices. Any African country that is still flirting with pseudo-one-party states or president-for-life strategies is in for a rude awakening. The gale of voter power is on an unstoppable march in Africa. The armies of organized opposition parties, local civil society organizations, independent print and electronic media and international election observers are steadily perfecting strategies that will allow citizens take back their governments in Africa.

Change can be peaceful. Perhaps, this is the most remarkable lesson from the 2002 Kenyan elections. from an entrenched ruling part to a spirited Opposition is now possible, without military, religious or international community intervention. In this regard, everybody must commend Ex-President Moi for his speedy, graceful and peaceful transfer of power to the new government.

Conclusion

In ending, I will give an unsolicited advice to President Kibaki, who finally became president on the third attempt: the problem of power is how to achieve its responsible use rather than its irresponsible and indulgent use - of how to get men of power to live for the public rather than off the public. These are the immortal words of Robert F. Kennedy. The people of Kenya have spoken. The ball is now in President Kibaki's court.

CHAPTER 15

LIBERIA: THE FAILURE OF AFRICAN AND UNITED STATES' LEADERSHIP

(July, 2003)

For the past few days, I have looked repeatedly at the picture shown by BBC and other news agencies of the young man carrying his probably pre-teen dead daughter on his back after her death from the ongoing madness in Liberia. For that young man, life may never be pure and legitimate again. As I look at the picture, one thing clearly comes to mind: the failure of African leaders and President George Bush to end the madness in Liberia. A bloodthirsty tyrant in the guise of a president has literally pushed that once peaceful and proud country into an unimaginable abyss since 1989. Charles Taylor has been an unmitigated disaster for his people. That young man in the BBC picture and his dead daughter dangling on his shoulders represent the present inability of Africa to resolve its problems in a timely fashion.

During President Bush's visit to Africa, and when he had landed in Nigeria, the BBC World News TV program has asked me what I thought of the situation in Liberia. I indicated that I was surprised that President Bush had not sent an emergency peacekeeping force to save lives in Monrovia, especially in view of the historical relationship between US and the United States. It is still unfortunate that President Bush is yet to deploy a peacekeeping force to Liberia.

However, my greatest regret is that once again, Africa is showing that it cannot preempt, manage or solve its problems. Since 1989, Charles Taylor and his acolytes have been at the root of most inter- and intra-state wars in West Africa. Since his "election" as president in 1997, Charles Taylor has run a state based on fear, primordial terror tactics, and plunder of government resources. Yet

Charles Taylor became a regular member of the presidents' club in both West Africa and Africa. In addition, Charles Taylor, in the spirit of the times, became a "born again" leader while state sanctioned killings, abductions and disappearances continued unabated. From time to time, again in line with the times, Charles Taylor mouthed off regarding his "belief" in democracy, the rule of law and globalization. In the theatre of the absurd, Charles Taylor is a high priest.

Today, hundreds of Liberians have died and many more will die in the coming days because of one individual. Many young men and women will once again hurriedly bury their fathers, mothers or children because African leaders cannot chase a diabolical tyrant from office. Tomorrow, many children will succumb to Cholera and other highly avoidable diseases in Liberia because Africa is still waiting for the West to solve its problems.

Will Liberia be free after the inevitable exit of Charles Taylor? You had better hold your breath. All the usual suspects who have contributed to the suffering of Liberia are now circling the wagons. These individuals include "Prince" Yormie Johnson and Roosevelt Johnson. Others are more sophisticated with their fancy degrees and Western connections. As far as these "leaders" are concerned, the race is on once again to become the "president" or "vice president" of Liberia. The long term suffering of Liberians is not an immediate issue. What is important is the consolidation of power, bringing "stability" and "respect" to Liberia and enthroning "democracy" or, if I may so suggest, the African version "demo crazy."

African leaders and their wannabes perfectly understand that there is very little retribution or justice for abominable acts in the continent. As Liberian "leaders" gather to wine and dine during "national" "conferences," plan for impending "elections" and plot on how to occupy the palatial and opulent presidential mansion that Charles Taylor will soon vacate, there is no guarantee that in two or three years ordinary Liberians will not be running for their lives in the streets of Monrovia or seeking shelter in the increasingly unsafe American Embassy as "new" rebel movements emerge from the shadows.

In Liberia as in most parts of Africa, the average Liberian is a pawn in the chessboard of the country's unrepentant leaders who have little faith or regard for the sacred covenant between the ruler and the ruled. The immediate and remote issues that led to Master Sergeant Doe's military coup are unlikely to be a major preoccupation of the Liberian elite as they celebrate Charles Taylor's exit and plot their way to power. Again, the next Liberian republic may come to fruition without any serious attempt to resolve critical national and county issues in Liberia.

I call on Liberians in the Diaspora, many of whom have suffered a lot in their host countries, to come together and salvage their country as soon Charles Taylor moves into exile. The biggest mistake Liberians in the Diaspora can ever make is to allow the likes of Charles Taylor or his fellow-travelers to terrorize their beloved country once again. Liberians in the Diaspora should work closely with those that stayed behind to choose political and economic leaders that will restore the cradle of Africa's democracy to its rightful place.

CHAPTER 16

WHY THE DARFUR TRAGEDY IS LIKELY To HAPPEN AGAIN

(July, 2004)

The unfolding tragedy in the western province of Sudan known as Darfur has gained the attention of the international community for the last several weeks. According to news reports, at least 50,000 black Africans of Darfur have died from a systematic orgy of bloodletting conducted by an Arab government-backed militia known as Janjaweed. The well-armed militia is reportedly conducting a government-sponsored ethnic cleansing campaign to drive away their black-skinned neighbors from their ancestral farming and grazing lands. More than one million people have fled their homes and are now nervously huddled in rain and wind swept makeshift refugee camps in Western Sudan and Chad.

As the usual wheels of continental and international diplomacy turn to end the tragedy in Darfur, I am afraid that nothing is in the offing to prevent another Darfur occurring in Sudan or any part of Africa in the immediate future. The high profile visits by world leaders to Darfur have done nothing to address key fundamental issues about this unfolding tragedy.

The Role of the Government of Sudan

Is the Sudanese government supporting an ethnic cleansing campaign against its citizens? Providing an immediate answer to this question is as important as rushing food aid to the refugees since you cannot rely on a complicit government to solve an inhumane condition it created in the first place. If the government is culpable, what are the specific consequences for its leaders and supporters?

The Role of the African Union

If the Sudanese government is conducting an ethnic cleansing campaign, should the African Union have a dialogue with this government and its leaders? What level of killings and population displacements will trigger deployment of military forces by the African Union to Darfur?

The Role of Western Countries

Should America and Britain have a dialogue with a government that is widely believed to be waging a war of ethnic hatred and murder against its citizens? Should the U.S. and Britain continue to explore mineral resources – especially oil – and possibly enrich/strengthen the leaders of a government waging a murderous campaign against selected citizens of its country? Should the U.S. and Britain rule out forceful intervention in Darfur to end a possible, unfolding genocide?

The United Nations and Multilateral Agencies

If a government decides to eliminate a select group of its citizens, should the UN and its agencies deal with that government on an "as usual" basis? When will the UN decide that the government has failed its people? What form of government-sanctioned atrocity will trigger the UN to seek alternative ways of managing a very grave humanitarian situation without passing though a complicit host government? Besides selective or "smart" economic sanctions targeted at elites of developing countries, what else should the UN do to stop a culpable government from selectively killing its own people?

Why Darfur will Occur Again

Darfur is likely to occur again because of the inability of African leaders and Western governments to develop and implement specific safeguards against ethnic cleansing and genocide. Ten years after the Rwanda genocide, the inability of African and Western leaders to develop and enforce safeguards against future ethnic cleansing and genocide have come full circle. What are these possible safeguards?

117

The first is to punish those that conceive, design, refine, implement and execute ethnic cleansing campaigns and genocide. If the leaders of the Sudanese government are found liable for the Darfur ethnic cleansing campaign, they must be brought to justice whether they pledge to turn over a new leaf, cooperate with the war on global terrorism, or voluntarily leave office. Sudanese academics, technocrats and religious leaders that provided support for ethnic cleansing must face justice. The leaders and backers of the Janjaweed militia (political, financial and technical) must also be brought to justice.

If rebels that support the black African population of Darfur committed acts of ethnic cleansing, they should be brought to justice as well. There should be zero tolerance for ethnic cleaning or genocide no matter the scale or attempted justification.

Second, African leaders and the African Union must demonstrate in very clear, unambiguous terms the end of any form of political and economic sanctuary for any government that by acts of omission or commission allows ethnic cleansing to occur within its jurisdiction. African nations and the African Union should act decisively on reports of ethnic cleansing and genocide, including but not limited to using military force to save lives. The Darfur tragedy is a litmus test for African leaders and the African Union.

Third, Western governments, especially the G-8 nations, should pay special attention to conflict and post-conflict states in Africa. Within the G-8 nations the U.S., Britain and France wield considerable influence in Africa and should lead this effort. G-8 nations can assist these states by investing significant human and material resources to seek political solutions to conflicts; to strengthen democratic principles and practices in these states by investing substantially in democratic and legal institutions; and to drastically reduce the economic burden of these impoverished states through debt forgiveness or drastic debt reduction, investing savings from debt relief on health, education and other social programs, and creating enabling environments for private enterprises. Western governments should also stop supporting governments that oppress their citizens in Africa.

Fourth, the UN and its agencies must now think the unthinkable – how to bypass murderous governments in any part of the world and reach its suffering citizens in a timely fashion. This will require a drastic review of how the UN and its agencies conduct business. If the government of Sudan is directly or tacitly encouraging ethnic cleansing in Darfur, the UN must devise ways of saving lives, isolating the leadership of that government, and seeking justice for the thousands of dead Sudanese whose only crime is the color of their skin. Rather than "smart" sanctions that makes everybody feel good but is often a slap on the wrist of the elite in developing countries, the UN may have to consider expelling countries whose governments are implicated in ethnic cleansing and genocide. The expelled country may be readmitted when the perpetrators of the ethnic cleansing and genocide leave office and face justice.

Fifth, the international community must support freedom of press and the free operation of civil society in developing countries. Without the constant news reports by the media, ethnic cleansing might have gone unnoticed in Darfur. To stop ethnic cleansing and genocide, it is crucial for the international community to support press freedom and an active civil society in developing nations as watchdogs of government activities.

As we ponder the next steps regarding Darfur, it is important to remember the young mothers in the refugee camps in Western Sudan and Chad. Some of these mothers are keeping vigil over surviving children who are gravely ill with diarrhoea or other diseases. These mothers may have lost their husbands, their children, their in-laws, and their own siblings. They may have lost their lifelong friends. Their only crime is the color of their skin and the murderous intentions of powerful people in positions of responsibility.

We must ensure that the sufferings of these mothers will not be in vain. Those responsible for the avoidable plight of these young mothers must never escape the long arm of justice. The Darfur tragedy should never happen again. However, we can only prevent a future Darfur with the development and enforcement of verifiable safeguards against ethnic cleansing and genocide. It can no longer be business as usual.

CHAPTER 17

DARFUR: A DEFINING MOMENT FOR AFRICAN LEADERS

With George Haley and Sidi Jammeh
(October, 2004)

As the ethnic based tragedy in Darfur, Western Sudan, continues to unfold despite a flurry of international and regional activities, the capacity of African leaders to prevent and manage avoidable conflicts is coming under close scrutiny.

Black African Muslims of Darfur have reportedly come under systematic bloody attacks by their Arab brethren. The United Nations estimates that up to 50,000 African Muslims of Darfur have died at the hands of an Arab militia known as Janjaweed, reportedly backed by the government of Sudan. More than a million Muslim Africans are now in refugee camps in Western Sudan and the neighboring country of Chad. This tragedy comes at a time when African leaders have developed a credible continental development strategy (the New Partnership for Africa's Development, NEPAD) and also repositioned its umbrella political organization, the African Union, to focus on good governance, economic prosperity, peace and political stability.

However, the Darfur tragedy has the capacity to undo this new vision of Africa where people of all ethnic nationalities and religious beliefs are working together to tackle the major problems of poverty and disease prevalent in many parts of this great continent. The fact that even a common religious belief could not spare Africans of Darfur from targeted killings and displacement from their ancient lands is even more troubling. It suggests a deep-rooted belief that ethnic cleansing could become a viable means of settling political, economic and cultural differences.

Domestic and international print electronic media have published eyewitness accounts of the staggering suffering inflicted on the Africans of Darfur. The latest report to the United Nations Security Council on October 5, 2004, by the Secretary General's envoy to Sudan, indicates that the government of Sudan over the past month has stood by watching while violence continued unabated in Western Darfur. Teachers and other educated elite people have faced targeted attacks. Despite international relief efforts, life in refugee camps remains grim and desperate. Young nursing mothers in refugee camps are not sure whether they can breastfeed their infants because of hunger and malnutrition. Outbreaks of communicable diseases are common.

The latest effort to broker peace in Sudan at Abuja between the Sudanese government and rebel movements representing black Africans of Darfur, under the auspices of the current chairman of the African Union, President Obasanjo of Nigeria, ended without much progress. The United Nations' deadline for the government of Sudan to take action in Darfur expired on August 30, 2004, without any consequences for the government. According to media reports, the Janjaweed militia continues to roam free, with a license to kill and maim.

We believe that to end ethnic-based killings in Darfur and prevent further suffering of black Muslims, African leaders and the African Union must show strong leadership and resolve in bringing the government of Sudan to order. Until now, African leaders and the African Union have shied away from directly confronting a government that is widely believed to be enforcing a deliberate policy of forcibly expelling its own citizens from their ancestral lands, repossessing such lands, and possibly, settling them with other more acceptable ethnic populations.

African leaders and the African Union are yet to hold the government of Sudan accountable for a potential genocide unfolding within its borders. The United States' Secretary of State, Colin Powell declared the ongoing tragedy in Darfur as genocide. It is important for the African Union to conduct its own investigation as soon as possible.

We do not believe that a continental policy of appeasement or business as usual in the United Nations will end a deliberate policy of targeted killings and forced movements of people from ancestral lands by a sitting government. We are yet to see any verifiable signs that the government of Sudan is ending its deadly policy in Darfur. Even the much-trumpeted intention to send a large contingent of 3,500 African peacekeepers to save lives in Darfur has stalled. Nigeria and Rwanda have reportedly sent about 300 peacekeepers to guard African Union monitors in Darfur.

Today, if we strip away all diplomatic posturing in Africa and at the United Nations, black Africans of Darfur are not assured of any protection from death and destruction. More important, black Africans of Darfur are yet to receive protection from other African governments and institutions. Without mincing words, African leaders have not led on this issue.

What to do? First, the African Union should immediately send a large peacekeeping force to Darfur. A large peacekeeping contingent will save lives and prevent conditions that could lead to further outbreak of communicable diseases. An immediate deployment should not depend on the acquiescence of the Sudanese government. It should also not be predicated on any possible United Nations sanctions or further action from Western governments.

Nigeria, South Africa and Egypt, as leading proponents of the new vision for Africa and with strong armies, should contribute well-armed troops that can protect lives and stare down any armed force in Sudan intent on continued killing of innocent women and children. It would be a defining moment for the African Union to act first without waiting for the United Nations or Western governments. African leaders should be prepared to do whatever it takes to stamp out the roots of ethnic cleansing or genocide in the continent. African leaders of the past such as Kenneth Kaunda and Julius Nyerere, despite leading poor countries, stood firm and made incalculable sacrifices to fight the Apartheid regime of South Africa and provide safe heavens for fledgling political independence movements in Zimbabwe and Namibia.

Second, Western nations should immediately provide financial and logistics support for the African peacekeeping force in Darfur. The United States should lead in this effort with significant technical and logistic support. If the United States believes that genocide is ongoing in Darfur, then it has a special responsibility to assist African leaders and help end the pain and suffering of the people of Darfur. Britain as the former colonial power in Sudan should provide significant support to the African peacekeeping force. The prime minister of Britain is well known for his concern for Africa. We are encouraged by Tony Blair's recent visit to Sudan and the reported fruitful discussion with the leadership of Sudan. However, what the Africans of Darfur need is an end to targeted killings and expulsion, and justice for those that planned and perpetrated these attacks.

Third, the African Union should launch an investigation to determine if genocide is occurring in Darfur, identify those behind the policy and practice of genocide, delineate the role of the Sudanese government in the crisis, and determine the real masterminds of the Janjaweed militia. The African Union should act immediately on receipt of these findings by taking unusual steps to deal with the perpetrators and supporters of the tragedy in Darfur.

The recent appointment of a five member United Nations tribunal to investigate claims of genocide is a welcome development. However, it does not waive the responsibility of the African Union to conduct its own investigations, to move swiftly to punish perpetrators, and to ensure that acts of ethnic cleansing and genocide are never official or unofficial government policies anywhere in Africa.

Finally, African leaders should develop a verifiable and enforceable mechanism for preventing and managing ethnic cleansing in the continent. A major section of this mechanism should deal with justice for the victims. A comprehensive mechanism should also establish specific repercussions for the planners and perpetrators of ethnic cleansing or genocide anywhere in Africa.

The Darfur tragedy is the perfect opportunity for African leaders to lead. As the international community unites in its condemnation of the unfolding tragedy in Darfur, African leaders should know they have support of all individuals, institutions and governments that are committed to the sacredness of human rights and the sanctity of human lives. African leaders should know that the international community will support their efforts to enforce the inalienable right of citizens to participate in the political and economic development of their countries.

We cannot allow a situation where the color of one's skin is the sole determinant of whether you will die violently or be forcibly ejected from your ancestral land. If the tragedy of Darfur were treated as a "normal" crisis or a "misunderstanding" between ethnic groups, then the enemies of Africa's renaissance who do not believe in freedom of expression, political pluralism or economic prosperity would have the upper hand. Darfur could be a powerful metaphor of Africa's capacity to stare down evil thoughts, to stop murderous actions, and to deal decisively with the planners and perpetrators of orchestrated violence. The ball is in the court of African leaders and the African Union. Failure is an unthinkable option.

Index

Ordering this book and other books by Adonis & Abbey Publishers

Wholesale inquiries (UK and Europe):

Gardners Books Ltd
+44 1323 521777, email: custcare@gardners.com

Wholesale inquiries (US and Canada):
Ingram Book Company (ordering)
+1 800 937 8000, website: www.ingrambookgroup.com

Online Retail Distribution: All leading online retail outlets including www.amazon.co.uk , www.amazon.com www.barnesandnoble.com, www.blackwell.com

Shop Retail: Ask any good bookshop or contact our office: www.adonis-abbey.com

+44 (0) 20 7793 8893

Printed in the United Kingdom
by Lightning Source UK Ltd.
115602UKS00001B/112